LB
1050.5
U4

**Umans, Shelley.**
    Designs for reading programs. New York, Bureau of
Publications, Teachers College, Columbia University, 1964.

    x, 76 p. 23 cm.

    Includes bibliographies.

    1. Reading—Remedial teaching.   ɪ. Title.

LB1050.5.U4           428.4               64—7853

# DESIGNS FOR READING PROGRAMS

# DESIGNS

# FOR  READING  PROGRAMS

Shelley Umans

**TEACHERS COLLEGE PRESS**

Teachers College, Columbia University
New York, 1964

In memory of my mother
Dorothy R. Barnett

# FOREWORD

In his now famous recommendations for reforms in teacher education, James B. Conant emphasized our need for "clinical professors" in education. A clinical professor is one who in addition to mastering the theories and findings of research in a field has acquired a high degree of professional skill. In his keynote address before the annual convention of the International Reading Association in 1962, Donald Durrell called for more "teacher professors." Other reading specialists have voiced the need, especially during this present period of clamor for change, of persons who have enjoyed a wide range of experience and reached a high level of sagacity in planning reading programs in all their practical details.

Shelley Umans is such a person. She has worked in every phase of teaching reading and planning reading programs in the New York City school system, which includes schools and neighborhoods of almost every kind. She has studied and taught in educational and reading clinics in public schools and colleges. She has served as a consultant to school systems all over the country. She has worked with many organizations seeking to try out new ventures in teaching reading.

That Shelley Umans has achieved a remarkable degree of practical insight and judgment is apparent in every page of this book. Something else is equally obvious. It is her ability to write with extraordinary clarity and brevity. In seventy-five pages she deals sensibly and sharply with the important issues faced by anyone undertaking to improve a reading program.

Arthur I. Gates

# CONTENTS

# DESIGNS FOR READING PROGRAMS

# PLANNING A SCHOOLWIDE

# READING PROGRAM

From the day he enters school every child should be provided with the means to achieve maximum development in accordance with his needs and ability. In order to assure the student a continuous, systematic plan of reading instruction, all members of the professional staff should play an important part in creating and carrying on a schoolwide reading program.

Suppose the principal asks you—reading consultant or reading teacher—to help organize the schoolwide reading program. He might say, in effect, "I'm disturbed about our school reading achievement scores. Although many students do well, their teachers feel they could do better. On the other hand, far too many of our students do poorly—really poorly, and still others seem completely lost. Moreover, I'm disturbed from another point of view. The librarian tells me that circulation has not increased over a two-year period, and she wonders about the reading interests of our students. How do we go about setting up a really varied and stimulating reading program in this school to reach as many students as possible? What is our first step?"

Perhaps the first step is to ask the principal if you and he together could explore the reading program in the school with the teachers. The classroom teacher, who is the one directly responsible for the child's learning more than anyone else in the school, knows the problems encountered in the classroom. An economical way of speaking to all teachers is to call a general conference to discuss a schoolwide reading program. More often than not, at such a conference, the teachers will take the initiative in expressing the specific needs of such a program. In turn, they will want to know how much direction and help they will get from you and from the principal. Teachers are interested in various classroom organizations, appropriate instructional materials, and new methods or approaches to instruction.

Once they are assured that direction and assistance are forthcoming, you might suggest that they select representatives to sit with you and the principal on a reading advisory council. This group will, in effect, develop the reading program for the school.

## DETERMINE STUDENT ABILITIES

In planning a schoolwide reading program, the reading advisory council would need to decide which students need remedial reading; which should be recommended for clinical services; and which should continue in a developmental reading program. This is not to imply that most schools do not have differentiated reading programs. However, it is very often accomplished by a teacher within a class or teachers on a grade. A school reading advisory council has the opportunity of looking at the total school reading program.

To help in making decisions as to the placement of students, the council should examine test results, both standardized and informal, and consult the classroom teacher on individual pupil achievement.

## ASSESS STAFF COMPETENCIES

The next step would be to assess the competencies of the staff so as to know which teachers work most effectively in the different phases of the reading improvement program. In the elementary schools, all teachers are expected to teach developmental reading. Because of temperament and special education, some may be better suited to work with students who have special reading problems. In the secondary schools, it may be found that few teachers within the school organization have been prepared in their preservice education to teach any type of reading —remedial or developmental. In this case, the reading consultant would institute an in-service program to include demonstrations, workshops, and conferences. No matter how well intentioned or well organized a program may be, it will fail unless the teachers feel secure in their ability to teach.

## DECIDE ON CLASS ORGANIZATION

After students have been classified and teachers, with the help of the reading teacher and the principal, have chosen their area of competency, the next step would be to decide on class (group) organization. Do you plan to provide for reading instruction during the regular class meeting, during special periods set aside for reading improvement, during extra periods added to special subject periods, during a concentrated part of the school term? Will instruction be given individually, in small groups, or in a combination of these class organizations? These decisions will depend in large part on how much time the staff is prepared to devote and on the administration's willingness to experiment with flexible grouping.

## PLAN THE PROGRAM

The next and perhaps the most important step is to plan the instructional program. Will you operate within the existing curriculum or are you planning a revision of the curriculum? What methods will you employ—the basal reader, programed instruction, self-selection? What instrumentation, if any, will be used in the program? Is there adequate space for the type of organization you are considering—large areas for grouping several classes together, small intimate areas for groups of five or six students, rooms for remedial reading?

Difficulties in organizing a reading program are no different from those in any other instructional area. Problems of outmoded buildings, overcrowded curricula, staffing, and diversity of students' needs should not deter the principal and reading teacher from adopting imaginative and creative approaches to a schoolwide reading program.

# THE DEVELOPMENTAL READING PROGRAM

A developmental reading program can mean different things to different people. It is hard to find a group of reading specialists who will agree on a single definition of "developmental." Therefore, in order to establish a frame of reference, let us use the following definition: A *developmental program* is one in which students who are able readers continue to be taught reading skills in a sequential program of instruction, designed to reinforce and extend the skills and appreciations acquired in previous years, and to develop new skills as they are needed. A developmental reading program should emphasize the development of reading power and guide students in the selection of reading materials.

Developmental reading starts in the kindergarten and continues through the high school years. In the elementary schools, reading is part of the curriculum and is taught by all teachers. A reading skills period may be scheduled for a specific time, but the competent teacher is aware of the need to apply the skills in every lesson throughout the school day. In the secondary school, skillful English language arts teachers assume most of the responsibility for the teaching of reading. However, in programing a school for developmental reading, every teacher (regardless of subject specialty) should be responsible for the teaching of reading in the classroom.

The effectiveness of a developmental reading program will depend on (1) the goals set by the staff; (2) the competency of the staff in carrying out these goals; (3) imaginative programing to provide for the best use of teacher and student time.

## DETERMINING READING ACHIEVEMENT

### Standardized Tests

The first step in setting up a developmental reading program is to determine the general reading achievement of the student. Skills, materials, and grouping procedures will all depend on the individual student's ability. In order to determine achievement, most school systems give standardized reading tests. These tests can be of value in helping to identify pupils who are above or below the class or grade average. Properly used, these tests can be of assistance in placing students in classes or in groups within classes. They can be misused when teachers fail to recognize that differences may exist between a student's ability to comprehend meaning in a selection and his ability to recognize isolated words, that a high score in one section of a test may elevate the total score, thus concealing low achievement in other sections of the test, and that the score on a standardized test is an indication of a student's frustration level (that level at which he has not been able to answer any more questions correctly) and not of the level at which he can cope with classroom instructional materials. Therefore, although standardized tests are used to determine reading ability, it must be remembered that they do not indicate the student's instructional or functional reading ability but merely his "maximum" performance on a reading test.

### Open Textbook Test

A more useful estimate of a student's instructional level is achieved through an informal test. An open textbook is probably the simplest type of informal test to administer, although it must be given individually. A series of graded textbooks such as a basal reading series may be used on the third, fourth, fifth, sixth, and seventh grade levels. A passage of equal length in each text should be selected. In administering and interpreting an informal textbook test:

1. Estimate the student's reading level and ask him to read a passage of about 100 words in a book that is one year below your estimate.

2. Ask the pupil to read orally without previous silent reading.
3. Count the errors as follows:
   a. Count as nonrecognition word errors all words which pupil does not know or mispronounces. Tell him the unknown word after five seconds but count as error.
   b. Count additions (words that pupil puts in) and omissions (words that pupil leaves out) as errors.
   c. Count as one type of error if pupil leaves off endings such as *s, ing,* or *ed.*
   d. Count the same error only once.
4. Interpret as follows:
   a. If pupil makes about five errors, assume the passage is at his true or functional reading level.
   b. If the pupil makes fewer than five errors, try a passage on the next higher grade level.
   c. If the pupil makes more than five errors, try a passage on the next lower grade level.
5. After the student has read the passage, ask two or three questions to test his comprehension. If the student has not understood what he has read, try a passage on the next lower grade level.

Such a test reveals a student's competencies by his ability to read approximately 95 per cent or more of the running words in a selection, and it tests his ability to understand what he has read. It also serves as an excellent diagnostic instrument by which to observe his reading mannerisms—finger pointing, head and lip movements, or facial and other tensions; his ability to read the material orally in rhythmic patterns (correct phrasing); his ability to interpret punctuation and to anticipate meaning; his ability to use word analysis techniques when necessary; and his ability to read silently at a rate considerably greater than his oral rate.

### Diagnosis by Teachers

With the general information given by a standardized test, the more specific information given by an informal textbook test, and the invaluable information given by a teacher observing a student's reading mannerisms, the student is now ready to be placed in the proper class.

## SELECTING PATTERNS OF ORGANIZATION

Let us assume the goals have been set by the faculty, that competent staff members have been chosen to participate in the program, and that the reading achievement of the students has been determined. That leads us, then, to the problem of deciding on the type of class organization to be employed. You, as the reading teacher or consultant, should be in the best position to suggest a variety of plans and programs.

Will the plan you select work? That will depend on the appropriateness of the plan to the needs of the students, on the depth of involvement of the classroom teacher, and on the interest, knowledge, and competency of the person initiating the program.

What will happen if the plan does not work? Little harm is done by ineffective programs if they are checked early enough. This calls for constant alertness on the part of the teacher, the reading consultant, and the school administration, coupled with a sound program of on-going evaluation.

What if the plan does work? The important questions then are *why* does it work and *for whom* does it work? When some of the answers to these qusetions are found, then the program may be extended.

### The Conventional Plan

Before we go into variations, let us take a look at the conventional plan that most schools employ. Generally, all the students are taught reading by their regular classroom teacher (in the secondary school the English language arts teacher is the reading teacher for the grade). These classes may be heterogeneous or homogeneous in reading ability, often depending on the size of the school. In large schools, classes may be formed on the basis of reading achievement, which, in itself, has limitations. In smaller schools—where there are just a few classes on each grade level—students may be placed in classes regardless of reading achievement. Whether students are placed in a heterogeneous or homogeneous classroom setting, reading achievement will, of course, vary within the class. In order to make provision for differences in reading ability, teachers usually form ability groups within the class and plan a reading program for each group. The poor readers work to develop basic skill in reading. The students above grade level may work in independent reading groups, in which a great variety of books is made available in order to sustain the interest of these better readers. The "normal ability" group would continue to learn the sequential reading skills.

There are times when a lesson should be given to the class as a whole, but more often instruction would be differentiated according to the students' abilities and interests. If a class is organized in which the ability of students is fairly homogeneous, the need for multiple grouping is somewhat lessened, but not by any means eliminated.

What are some of the limitations of this plan? First, if the teacher forms too many groups, the teaching may become confused and learning doubtful, since faulty grouping can actually impede instruction. Secondly, it assumes that all reading skills can be provided for in group activities. As reading teachers, we know that this is not possible. Reading skills are learned in every aspect of the instructional program. Thirdly, such a plan assumes that each teacher is competent in all aspects of the teaching of reading, and little provision is made for the varying individual differences among teachers.

Before selecting a group pattern, the teacher should have in mind the purposes of the group. What is to be accomplished by forming a group—why not a whole-class lesson? He must then assess his own competency in handling groups. Only a highly skilled teacher can control more than two groups at a time in a class and still give adequate instructional attention to all groups. There have been many studies of the effect of grouping on learning. The results are conflicting. Whereas some prove that ability groups have merit, others prove that pupils learn more in heterogeneous groups. Perhaps these reports conflict because of the one variable that cannot be measured: namely, the intensity of the desire of the teacher to make a group plan work effectively.

No plan will suit the needs of all the students in the school, and each plan will have to be adapted to the abilities of the student body and to the competencies of the professional staff. In considering the use of any organizational plan, one must consider not only its advantages and the limitations but also the possible alternatives. The following plans are deviations from the conventional self-contained classroom organization.

## Special Reading Achievement Classes

In this organization, all pupils are assigned to special reading classes during some part of the regular school day. Pupils are grouped for special periods according to reading achievement and regardless of grade placement. A student in the fourth grade may be reading with a sixth-grade class if he has the skill to read the more advanced selections and, conversely, a sixth-grade student may be reading with fourth-grade readers if such is his ability. The number of students in each reading class may vary. Students who can move rapidly may be taught in large groups, whereas those who need a great deal of reinforcement may be taught in smaller groups. This program allows for mobility of students during the school year. A student who is making rapid progress may be moved into the next level without having to change his homeroom class. Another student may spend several periods with a reading group other than the one to which he is regularly assigned because that group may be concentrating on areas of reading in which he needs special instruction. This cannot be done in the conventional self-contained classroom.

Unlike the conventional plan, this plan attempts more workable provision for students with varying reading abilities. We know, of course, that narrowing the reading range of a class does not insure more successful learning, but it does make the group more teachable from the standpoint of materials and skills taught.

This plan, however, has certain limitations. Placing children with advanced reading abilities in classes with older children presumes common interests. This may not be so, and the younger learner might suffer from "feeling different." Also, unless this plan is tightly structured, continuity of learning may suffer if children are moved too often from group to group. Teachers, also, may find it difficult helping students "fit" into ongoing programs. Nevertheless, the question of how real these problems are should be reevaluated. Perhaps certain factors that we think will hamper growth may, in reality, stimulate and challenge children.

## Subject Area Skills Plan

Another plan that shows promise is the *subject area skills plan*. In this arrangement, students are assigned to extra reading periods in each subject area. In the elementary school, the extra time may be found by shortening certain periods or by substituting reading instruction for less important activities. In the secondary school, if no other area of the curriculum can be eliminated, extra periods for reading instruction may come from electives.

An example of scheduling subject area reading is to assign students to two periods a week for the express purpose of learning reading skills in addition to the regularly scheduled number of periods assigned for English. In social studies, mathematics, and science, an additional period may be assigned for the special purpose of learning the reading skills of each subject. Each content area teacher, therefore, takes the responsibility for teaching the reading skills in his subject.

An imaginative principal or program chairman may use varying types of classroom organizations to implement this plan. For example, in the secondary school a mathematics teacher might have three of his classes scheduled to meet at the same hour for large-group instruction in the reading skills of mathematics. In this way the teacher avoids repeating a lesson to each group, and it allows him time to work in the other periods with small groups of students who need more intensive help. This can be done in almost any subject area. In the elementary school, a similar large-group plan might be developed with one teacher taking the responsibility for reading skills in a given subject while another combines classes to teach other subject area skills.

One of the advantages of this plan is that specific periods are set aside for the teaching of reading. Too often, despite all good intent, reading instruction becomes deferred when integrated in the subject period. Reading skills may be applied and reinforced during regular instruction, but the actual introduction of the skill may be most effectively presented in a time unit specifically assigned for that purpose. This plan gives time for systematic developmental reading instruction within each subject area.

The plan, however, may present problems to the subject teacher. With the ever-expanding content of each subject area, there is little enough time to cover the curriculum without adding reading skills to the already crowded course of study. It should be brought to the attention of the teacher that the learning of content will be facilitated if the student has the specific skills with which to read and understand the subject matter. In addition, it may be found that elementary school teachers as well as secondary subject specialists are reluctant to teach specific subject area reading skills because they do not have adequate training. A reading consultant or a well-trained supervisor or teacher can be an invaluable aid in overcoming this objection through an in-service teacher education program.

### Departmental Reading Plan

Another plan that could be used in both elementary and secondary schools is the *departmental reading plan*. In this arrangement, the school year is divided into four ten-week sections. One of these sections may be devoted to typewriting, another to fine arts, another to industrial arts, and still another to reading. Each student is assigned to each one of these sections at different times throughout the school year. For each of the ten-week periods, the students meet one hour each day. This concentrated approach has the advantage of sustaining student interest while offering a comprehensive and intensive program in each of these areas. In reading, every student (regardless of his reading skill) receives instruction from the reading specialist at some time during the school year. For example, in the first ten-week section, the reading specialist may meet four classes of students with reading disabilities (remedial reading) and, in the second ten-week section, four classes of normal readers (developmental reading). The third section might be the same as the second (developmental reading) and the fourth section reserved for those students who are advanced readers (gifted class). However, for those who still have reading problems after the ten-week session, provision should be made to continue working with them throughout the year with a scheduled but less intensive course.

The major limitation of this plan is that unless the classroom teacher is involved in observing some of the ten-week lessons and in meeting in conference with the reading consultant, the program will have little follow-up. A ten-week "crash program" such as this is just an initial step. The major part of the program must take place in the classroom.

## PLANNING THE INSTRUCTIONAL PROGRAM

Comprehension is fundamental to success in reading. In order to understand what is being read, a pupil must first be able to recognize new words, to learn their meaning and pronunciation. He must also be interested in increasing his vocabulary. He must learn to comprehend sentences, paragraphs, and complete selections. Through reading, he should be able to revise or reinforce his attitudes and opinions. A balanced program of instruction should provide for these learnings.

The teaching of reading starts the first day a youngster enters kindergarten. He learns to hang his coat under the hook labeled with his name. He recognizes his teacher's name. He may learn to read the words "Boys," "Girls," even "Lunchroom." From this point on and for the rest of his life, he will be acquiring and refining reading skills. Let us take a look at "reading instruction."

### Beginning Reading

Most children today come to kindergarten with a background of experiences and a speaking vocabulary greater than those of children of a few years ago. Accordingly, materials that develop readiness for reading (picture books, books with easy vocabulary, matching games, story sequence games, story books for teachers to read aloud) are very important and must be selected with great care; they must reflect the changes in the readiness level of the students. Teacher-made materials or locally produced materials are particularly important in a reading readiness program. Children's personal experiences, charts which tell about trips, record-listening experiences, films, and stories are a few of these teacher-made materials.

For schools using a basal reader, it is suggested that materials be purchased in two or more reading series on each reading level. Pupils sometimes find it difficult to make the upward step from one reader to another in the same series; therefore, having materials (with similar vocabulary) from other publishers provides an additional resource for motivation in what may be the necessary intermediate step in reading progress. For this same purpose, many publishers market materials supplementary to their basic reading series.

In addition to the regular basal readers and workbooks, there should be an array of supplementary material such as reading kits, practice exercises, reading games, skill building stories, and magazines. These materials, while not complete programs in themselves, will enrich and broaden the regular program. But, perhaps most important of all, there must be books, books, and more books for the youngsters to read.

For schools using a self-selection or individualized reading approach, it is suggested that teachers be well trained in this approach and that large numbers of carefully chosen books be available. Basal readers are eliminated as the core of reading instruction, since they impose a uniform reading selection. This program offers the opportunity for the child to select his own reading material. In the self-selection program, children have access to many more books in keeping with their interest. There should be a minimum of ten trade books per child, suited, of course, to his reading and interest levels. In addition to trade books, magazines, newspapers, and dictionaries, there should be available copies of appropriate textbooks in all curriculum areas. The teacher may use these when developing special reading skills.

Under the teacher's guidance, the student selects the book he wishes to read from a large variety of books. Periods are set aside for quiet and independent reading. During these periods, students are assigned an individual conference time with the teacher. At these conferences the teacher and the student discuss his reading, and specific skills are taught as the need is evidenced. The teacher uses a check list to record skills taught, books read, and progress noted. The stigma of being placed in a "low group" is removed as each student functions independently on his own level and "reading groups," as such, are not part of the program.

Even though the individual conference is an important component of the self-selection program, it is not its sole feature. Periods are set aside when pupils meet as a class for sharing and evaluating books they have read. The self-selection program offers high motivation because of the number and variety of books available to the student. It also fulfills the universal desire of a student to have a time "of his own" with the teacher. There is much to commend this program. Articles and books describing the self-selection program in detail are available.[1]

[1] See, for example, Leland B. Jacobs *et al.*, *Individualized Reading Practices* (New York: Bureau of Publications, Teachers College, Columbia University, 1958); and Jeannette Veatch (ed.), *Individualized Reading* (New York: G. P. Putnam's Sons, 1959).

However, the self-selection program raises a number of questions as to its effectiveness for universal use in schools. Can every teacher with thirty students in a class find sufficient time for individual conferences that will provide for careful evaluation and instruction? Can a teacher realistically keep detailed records for each student, which will allow for teaching systematic sequences of reading skills? How much reading is done by the slow learner who cannot read fluently and therefore cannot read extensively? Can every classroom be provided with an abundant supply of books within the interest and ability ranges of the students? Are most teachers sufficiently familiar with children's literature to be able to help them in selecting books?

So far, research has told us little about the effectiveness of this program. Most of the research has been too limited in scope and too uncontrolled to prove anything conclusively.

### Sequential Learning of Skills

Although the reading act itself involves using many skills at one time, the teaching of *certain skills must naturally precede others* (whether a basal reading approach or a self-selection approach is involved) if the student is to read effectively. Although a teacher does not wait to teach structural analysis until the child has "mastered" all phonetic analysis skills (and 220 basic sight words), a knowledge of a number of sight words and an ability to pronounce words is necessary in order to be able to divide words into syllables and to study their roots, prefixes, and suffixes.

Grace Goodell, a reading consultant in the New York City school system, has developed a "skill ladder" (see Figure 1, page 16) which may be used as a guide to teachers when planning a sequential developmental reading program. The advantage of this ladder is that it presents a gradeless approach to the teaching of required skills: that is, it does not confine the teacher to teaching specific skills in a particular grade. For example, if one group in the class has sufficient knowledge of basic sight words, that group is then ready to move on to phonetic analysis. Another group, fairly skilled in phonetic analysis, may be ready to work on structural analysis, and so on up the ladder. This does not, of course, preclude the constant teaching and reinforcement of all skills at all times. It merely places "emphasis."

## SKILLS LADDER

| | |
|---|---|
| *Step 13* | Using the Encyclopedia and Other Reference Books |
| *Step 12* | Using the Dictionary |
| *Step 11* | Using Parts of a Book |
| *Step 10* | Following Directions |
| *Step 9* | Inferring Meanings |
| *Step 8* | Classifying and Organizing Facts |
| *Step 7* | Finding the Supporting Details |
| *Step 6* | Finding the Main Idea |
| *Step 5* | Vocabulary Building |
| *Step 4* | Using Contextual Clues |
| *Step 3* | Using Structural Analysis |
| *Step 2* | Using Phonetic Analysis |
| *Step 1* | Basic Sight Words |

If a special need for a particular skill arises, regardless of its position in the skill ladder, a teacher can teach the skill at that time. In other words, although the order of the ladder is developmental, it need not be followed in sequence. The following pages present an analysis of the ladder, together with suggestions for its use.

*"Previous learning"* includes those skills needed before proceeding to the next step or *skill*. The *subskills* listed under each primary skill form the foundation for adequate understanding of, and functioning in, that skill. However, a teacher may select only those which are needed for and suited to the abilities of a particular group.

## STEP 2

**Previous learning**  basic sight words

**Skill**  *using phonetic analysis:* association of sounds with consonants and vowels

    a. auditory and visual perception of consonants: beginning, middle, ending

    b. auditory and visual perception of consonant blends

    c. auditory and visual perception of digraphs

    d. auditory and visual perception of vowels: long, short, with *r*, diphthongs, digraphs

    e. using visual clues to vowel sounds

    f. auditory and visual clues to rhyming elements: final parts have the same sound—look alike: snow/grow; look different: so/grow

    g. auditory perception of syllables: syllable ending with vowel sound; syllable ending with consonant sound; syllable ending with *le*

    h. auditory perception of accent

    i. using visual clues to accent

**STEP 3**

**Previous learnings**    basic sight words

using phonetic analysis

**Skill**    *using structural analysis:* identifying meaning units in words

    a. identifying base or root words

       1. inflectional variants formed by adding *s, d, ing* to known words

       2. compounds made up of two known root words

       3. compounds made up of one known and one unknown word

       4. inflected forms of known words in which *es, er, or, est, n,* or *en* is added to the root word

       5. inflected forms of words in which the last letter is changed before adding an ending—doubling the consonant, *y* changed to *i, f* to *v,* dropping final *e*

       6. derived forms of words in which prefixes or suffixes are added to the root word

       7. contractions in which one or two letters are omitted

    b. identifying pronunciation units or syllables following these principles

       1. if the first vowel sound in a word is followed by two consonants, the first syllable usually ends with the first of the two consonants—e.g., *but ter*

       2. if the first vowel sound in a word is followed by a single consonant, that consonant usually begins the second syllable—e.g., *ba by*

       3. if the last syllable of a word ends in *le* preceded by a consonant, that consonant usually begins the last syllable—e.g., *cra dle*

4. the syllable in a word often does not break between consonant blends or special two-letter consonant symbols —e.g., *hun gry, re claim*

5. in a word of more than one syllable, the letter *v* usually goes with the preceding vowel to form a syllable —e.g., *trav el*

*Note:* In word recognition, a combination of phonetic, structural, and contextual skills is used to unlock both pronunciation and meaning of a word. Therefore, the structural skills are developed within the framework of the total word recognition program.

## STEP 4

**Previous learnings**  basic sight words
using phonetic analysis
using structural analysis

**Skill**  *using contextual clues* for word recognition and meaning

a. inferring unknown word from pictured context

b. inferring unknown word from pictured and verbal context (later level includes maps, charts, diagrams, etc.)

c. inferring unknown word from verbal context alone

d. combining above context clues with visual clues (word form)

e. identifying specific context clues
1. definition with sentence
2. appositive phrase
3. typographical aids
4. synonyms and antonyms (words or phrases)
5. metaphors and similes
6. anticipating the meaning

f. selecting from multiple meanings
1. understanding that a word may have more than one meaning
2. selecting correct meaning

         3. checking selected meanings in context

      g. identifying special shades of meaning of a word

*Note:* In word recognition, a combination of phonetic, structural, and contextual skills is used to unlock both pronunciation and meaning of a word. Therefore, the contextual skills are developed within a framework of the total word recognition program.

## STEP 5

**Previous learnings**    basic sight words
                     using phonetic analysis
                     using structural analysis
                     using contextual clues

**Skill**            *vocabulary building*

    a. getting the precise meaning of familiar words in accordance with the intention of the context—e.g., *baste* in cooking and *baste* in sewing

    b. getting the meaning of the new words directly from the rest of the sentence

        1. when it can be anticipated from the rest of the sentence

        2. when there are positive clues in the context (definition)

        3. when there are negative clues in the context

        4. when there are a number of details in the context

    c. getting the meaning or checking the meaning of new words from glossary or dictionary

## STEP 6

**Previous learnings**    basic sight words
                     using phonetic analysis
                     using structural analysis
                     using contextual clues
                     vocabulary building

**Skill**                 *finding the main idea*
a. directly stated in first sentence
b. stated in the last sentence
c. stated in part of one sentence
d. where two sentences are used to express main idea
e. where it must be found within the body of the paragraph
f. where it must be inferred

## STEP 7

**Previous learnings**    basic sight words
using phonetic analysis
using structural analysis
using contextual clues
vocabulary building
finding the main idea

**Skill**                 *finding supporting details* to the main idea
a. where guide words are used
b. when details provide a listing or sequence of facts
c. when details illustrate main idea
d. when details prove or explain main idea
e. when supporting details contain sub-topics

## STEP 8

**Previous learnings**    basic sight words
using phonetic analysis
using structural analysis
using contextual clues
vocabulary building
finding the main idea
finding supporting details

**Skill**                 *classifying and organizing facts*
a. grouping objects according to common characteristics

    b. organizing names into related groups

    c. organizing ideas expressed as topics

*outlining*

    a. recognizing the purposes and need for outlining

    b. changing sentences to topics

       1. eliminating unnecessary words

       2. changing order of words, making minor changes

    c. seeing relationship between main topic and subtopics

       1. when clue words are given

       2. when events are listed in sequence

       3. when a comparison is indicated

    d. using an outline form

    e. outlining longer sections

       1. using author's organizational devices

       2. selecting broad topics from related topics

## STEP 9

**Previous learnings**   basic sight words
using phonetic analysis
using structural analysis
using contextual clues
vocabulary building
finding the main idea
finding supporting details
classifying and organizing facts; outlining

**Skill**   *inferring meanings*

    a. inferring meanings from pictorial clues

    b. inferring meanings of words from contextual clues

    c. inferring meaning of figures from speech

    d. inferring implied details

    e. reading "between the lines"

    f. inferring general significance of a paragraph

    g. predicting outcomes
    h. forming opinions

*reacting to reading*

    a. thinking critically
    b. reading with appreciation

## STEP 10

**Previous learnings**   basic sight words
using phonetic analysis
using structural analysis
using contextual clues
vocabulary building
finding the main idea
finding supporting details
classifying and organizing facts; outlining
inferring meanings; reacting to reading

**Skill**   *following directions*

    a. following a short list of directions
    b. following a longer list of directions

## STEP 11

**Previous learnings**   basic sight words
using phonetic analysis
using structural analysis
using contextual clues
vocabulary building
finding the main idea
finding supporting details
classifying and organizing facts; outlining
inferring meanings; reacting to reading
following directions

**Skill**   *using parts of a book*

    a. book cover, title page
    b. reverse side of title page
    c. table of contents
    d. lists of maps, illustrations, and tables
    e. preface
    f. chapter, sectional, paragraph, and marginal headings

    g. footnotes
    h. glossary
    i. bibliography
    j. appendices
    k. index

## STEP 12

**Previous learnings**  basic sight words
using phonetic analysis
using structural analysis
using contextual clues
vocabulary building
finding the main idea
finding supporting details
classifying and organizing facts; outlining
inferring meanings; reacting to reading
following directions
using parts of a book

**Skill**    *using the dictionary*

    a. knowing types of information offered by the dictionary
    b. finding words quickly
      1. knowing and using alphabetical arrangement
      2. finding right part of the dictionary
      3. using guide words
    c. finding the correct meaning of a word
      1. identifying and using synonyms, antonyms
      2. identifying and using definitions
      3. interpreting illustrations
      4. using cross references
      5. identifying and interpreting idioms
    d. using the dictionary as a pronouncer
      1. identifying and using syllabic divisions of words
      2. identifying and using preferred pronunciation
      3. interpreting accent marks
    e. using the dictionary as a speller

**STEP 13**

Previous learnings  basic sight words
using phonetic analysis
using structural analysis
using contextual clues
vocabulary building
finding the main idea
finding supporting details
classifying and organizing facts; outlining
inferring meanings; reacting to reading
following directions
using parts of a book
using the dictionary

**Skill**                 *using the encyclopedia and other reference
books*

a. recognizing specific purposes
b. arrangement of materials
c. using the index
d. using the visual aids
e. understanding purposes of various
types of encyclopedia
f. significance of date of publication

### Reading for Appreciation

There must be a high order of understanding before appreciation can be realized. In literature, understanding must precede appreciation. One must understand the characters, their changing personalities, their feelings and motives; and one must recognize how all these elements shape events which follow. One should decide whether or not the events are plausible. The student should become involved in, and respond to, experiences in a selection and relate the implications in his reading to his own thinking. This is the beginning of appreciation and it leads to the development of discriminating taste. Reading develops attitudes, concepts, and interests and presents a special challenge to the mind and the imagination. The content of literature provides material for that challenge.

The goals of reading for appreciation might be presented

in the form of a pyramid with each level of understanding built on a previous learning.

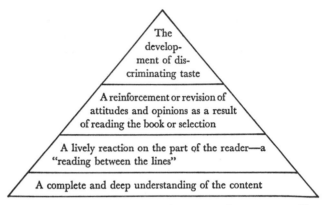

The *gifted child* is particularly responsive to a reading appreciation program if the program is well planned and presented with imagination and if the instructional materials are carefully selected. Gifted children should be guided to select books that are a challenge to their ability and understanding. They may be stimulated with questions that lead the mind into wider understanding and further questioning. Gifted children can read more books and accept more searching assignments than the average child. In addition to the appreciation skills discussed for the developmental reading program, the gifted child is interested in the history of words, the science of semantics, figurative language, and the effect of context on the meaning of words. A teacher must do more than merely surround these children with books; gifted children should be guided into the finer and more advanced reading appreciation skills.

*Oral reading* should be an integral part of the reading program in every grade for all children. Generally, it is well to have oral reading follow silent reading. Primarily, the aim of silent reading is *to get the thought;* the aim of oral reading is *to express the thought.* Among the many values of oral reading are the following:

1. It may reveal the mechanical difficulties encountered in silent reading.
2. Speech defects can be identified and corrective measures taken.
3. Comprehension can be sharpened by listening to the organization of the thoughts expressed.

4. Expression in reading can be developed, thus bringing added meaning to the selection.
5. Retention is strengthened by oral repetition.
6. A feeling of social communication is encouraged through oral reading.

A student may have many occasions for oral reading other than those arising in a school setting. He may, for example, want to read aloud to family or friends or read to inform or prove a point; he may read aloud to himself for appreciation, as in poetry; or he may read in concert.

When oral reading is used for diagnosis, it may reveal, to the careful observer, reading weaknesses and frustration levels. However, no pupil should be asked to read orally and before an audience materials that present substantial difficulty in word recognition. If a teacher uses oral reading for diagnostic purposes only, the passage should be short and the student should be alone with the teacher. Oral reading, as such, should be a successful and satisfying experience in communication.

### Efficient Reading: SQ3R and S-P-D Techniques

When students are asked in what area they would like to improve their reading, more often than not they will say they would like to read "faster." This, of course, is a misstatement. What they really mean is that they want to be able to adjust their reading rate (faster for some articles, slower for others) to the purpose for which they are reading the selection. For example, a scientist reading a research paper will read at a different rate from the one he would use when reading a newspaper. A student reading a social studies assignment should adjust his rate to his purpose; he will use one rate to survey the article and still another when reading it through for details.

Developmental reading programs should include instruction in adjusting reading speed. The first step, therefore, is for the student to survey the article he is to read to decide which parts of the article are to be read for exact information and which can be skimmed for general information. This helps the student to be "selective" as to the parts he reads.

Perhaps the most familiar survey technique is the SQ3R. "S" stands for *survey*. You look first to see if the chapter has a summary. If so, it should be read first. Then, topical headings are skimmed. The reader is attempting to get the total picture so that when he studies his assignment, details become more meaningful as they are related to the whole. His next step is to read the material, and he does this by changing the paragraph topics into *questions* ("Q"). He then reads in order to answer these questions. Of what value is this? It gives a purpose for reading. The learner is ready to begin work when he can state the problem in his own words. He is reading to find the answer to a question. It gives direction to his study. The learning situation is activated.

The first of the three "R"s refers to *reading*. Read to answer the question. Vary the kind of reading according to purpose. Often it is unnecessary to read slowly and carefully. Skimming may suffice. On occasion the reader may be quite familiar with the subject matter. At other times he will find the material difficult and technical. An important difference between good and poor readers is the ability to adjust skill to purpose. The latter read simple material as slowly and carefully as they would study a scientific treatise.

The second "R" is *recitation*. Recalling what has been read is one of the most effective ways to increase retention. We forget at a much more rapid rate immediately after a learning experience than at any other time. Reciting at this time also helps the reader to evaluate his understanding. He is able to direct this attention to specific points of difficulty for economy of effort.

The third "R" emphasizes spaced *review*. Review periods should come close together at first and then gradually further apart. They should be varied. New ways to apply the material will make it more meaningful and useful, in addition to increasing retention.

Another method of "surveying" material is the one used by the United States Department of Agriculture, the S-P-D approach —Survey-Preread-Decide. The steps are presented to students in the following manner:

"S"—*Survey*. Your first step in attacking any practical prose is to size up the task ahead and define your purpose for reading. You should ask yourself: What is all this about? Who wrote it? When? Why am I reading it? How long is it? How is it organized? What are its parts and subparts? Where are the introduction, the body, the ending? At the same time look for illustrations, graphs, tables, and clues to the author's style and the types of paragraphs he constructs. If the author has written a summary, you may want to read this first.

"P"—*Preread.* Let us say you are reading a short article, one you have surveyed and prepared yourself for reading, tentatively identifying the three main parts—the introduction, the body, and the ending. Your next steps are:

1. Read the introduction (first paragraph or two) rapidly.
2. Read the first sentence only of each succeeding paragraph until you reach the last paragraph or two. (Well-written paragraphs usually have a "main idea" sentence called the topic sentence. While the topic sentence may be located anywhere in the paragraph, most often it is the first sentence.)
3. Read the last paragraph or two rapidly.

At this point you should have a rather good outline of the author's message. You are now ready for the third step.

"D"—*Decide.* Several courses of action are open to you:

1. Skip. You may find that the article is not what you want. You may skip it or leave it unread.
2. Skim. You may decide that it contains a fact, name, date, or idea you can use. Your next step is to skim quickly over the print to locate what you want.
3. Read. You may decide that the article is important enough to read. If so, return to the beginning and read it thoroughly to fill in the ideas you missed in your prereading.
4. Study. Finally, you may decide that much of the article is worth remembering. You might then adopt a number of learning techniques such as underlining important ideas, making marginal notes, reciting to yourself, rereading parts, and even outlining the ideas or summarizing orally or in writing what you have read.

Now let us review the steps of the S-P-D approach:

1. "S"—*Survey.* Size up the material to be read. Make sure you know why you are reading and have some notion of what you hope to learn.
2. "P"—*Preread.* (*a*) Read first paragraph rapidly and fully. (*b*) Shift to reading first sentence only of following paragraphs. (*c*) Read the last paragraph fully.

3. "D"—*Decide* to (*a*) skip; (*b*) skim; (*c*) read; or (*d*) study.

At all times, in a survey method, the purpose for reading must be kept in mind and then the reader proceeds by the most efficient way to accomplish his purpose. Students should be taught that they will want to skip some materials altogether. With other materials, a rough idea of the content may be all they need. Finally, some materials they will want to understand thoroughly and perhaps commit to memory.

## SELECTING INSTRUCTIONAL MATERIALS

We are all aware that there is a marked relationship between children's reading success and the quality and appropriateness of the material. The selection of reading materials is a key to reading improvement. Numerous professional publications list instructional materials. Educational publishers are generally willing to discuss new materials with school personnel. However, no matter what materials are considered, there are certain guiding principles for the selection and ordering of instructional materials. These principles are as follows:

1. Materials should be up to date, in good physical condition, and available in sufficient quantities.
2. Keep in mind the type of instructional approach used in the school (e.g., basal readers, self-selection).
3. Fit your selections to the experience backgrounds of the students.
4. Consider special student groups, such as those with mature interests and low reading ability, or those with special interest areas and high ability.
5. Select materials suitable to such special classes as remedial reading, classes for the gifted, non-English speaking, classes for the mentally retarded.
6. Provide materials, if necessary, to meet the introduction of changes in the reading program by way of programed instruction, reading in the content fields, or self-selection reading.
7. Allow for proper allocation to classes and anticipated changes in enrollment.

# GUIDES TO
# DETERMINING READING ACHIEVEMENT

## In the Literature

Botel, Morton. *Predicting Readability Levels* (Chicago: Follett Publishing Co., 1962).

This is a simple and easy-to-use method of determining a readability score for a pupil with any reading material.

*Education for the Gifted.* 57th Yearbook of the National Society for the Study of Education, Part II (Chicago: University of Chicago Press, 1958).

Martin, John. "Using Test Results to Improve Reading Instruction," *National Elementary Principal*, Vol. 40, No. 7 (May 1961), pp. 43–44.

A description of expectancy formulae and how they can be used for instruction.

Sheldon, William D. "Reading Instruction in Junior High School." In *Development in and Through Reading.* 60th Yearbook of the National Society for the Study of Education, Part I (Chicago: University of Chicago Press, 1961), pp. 305–19.

Hints on ascertaining interests and potential reading abilities of candidates for junior high school developmental reading programs. Includes suggestions for methods and materials.

Taylor, Earl. "Grouping Pupils and Adults in Terms of Sight Vocabulary and the Fundamental Reading Skills," *Journal of Developmental Reading*, Vol. 5, No. 3 (Spring 1962), pp. 164–71.

Author claims that grouping according to data from eye movement photographs provides unusual possibilities.

## From the Schools

*Reading Inventories*
    Lakewood, Ohio—Elementary
    Bucks County (Doylestown), Pennsylvania—Elementary
    New York City—Junior high

*The Learning Methods Test* (available from Robert E. Mills, 319 S.E. 6th St., Fort Lauderdale, Florida)

An attempt is made through these tests to help the teacher determine a pupil's aptitude for learning by various instructional methods. Test may be given to groups or individuals.

## GUIDES TO
## SELECTING PATTERNS OF ORGANIZATION

### In the Literature

Bossone, R. M. "Principal's Role in the Reading Program," *Elementary English,* Vol. 40, No. 3 (March 1963), pp. 277–79.

Suggestions to principal on how to go about selecting and implementing a reading program in his school.

*Developmental Reading in the Content Areas.* Report of Proceedings, 1960 Spring Conference of Chicago Area Reading Association of the International Reading Association (Crane Campus, Chicago Teachers College, 1960).

A good article on "why" and "how to" initiate a content area reading skills program in the secondary school.

Early, M. "A High School Faculty Considers Reading," *The Reading Teacher,* Vol. 13, No. 4 (April 1960), pp. 282–87.

". . . caution may be a questionable virtue, but careless experimentation . . . may certainly be a deterrent to progress." Author asks that the entire high school faculty view critically the problems of teaching reading in the United States and then move ahead firmly toward their goals.

Goodlad, J. L. "What About Non-Grading Our Schools?" *The Instructor,* Vol. 70, No. 9 (May 1961), p. 64.

A plan for ungraded classes in the elementary school is described.

McCracken, Glenn. *The Right to Learn* (Chicago: Henry Regnery Company, 1959).

Report on 12-year-old "New Castle Experiment." A detailed description of the "tested method for improving reading." Primarily a phonic approach accompanied by teaching films.

Veatch, Jeannette. *Individualizing Your Reading Program* (New York: G. P. Putnam's Sons, 1959).

Part I includes description, direction, and philosophy of individualized reading. Part II presents eighteen programs described by the staffs, consultants, or supervisors who developed them.

### From the Schools

Daigle, Edward. "A Program of Developmental Reading," *Journal of Developmental Reading,* Vol. 6, No. 2 (Winter 1963), pp. 130–33.

Success with a developmental reading program in a vocational high school in a small Louisiana community.

DiBisasio, Anthony. "The Developmental Reading Program at Lakewood High School," *Journal of Developmental Reading,* Vol. 6, No. 1 (Autumn 1962), pp. 67–68.

Introduction, acceptance, and results of a developmental reading program designed for a 1700-pupil high school.

Harrocks, E. M. "Extending Reading Skills in a Large City System," *Proceedings,* International Reading Association Conference, Vol. 6 (1961), pp. 60–61.

Tells what is happening in the Cleveland area in reading instruction, with emphasis placed on Saturday workshops for reading teachers.

Warren, Mary. "The Massapequa Junior High School Reading Program," *Journal of Developmental Reading,* Vol. 5, No. 4 (Summer 1962), pp. 245–55.

Report on pilot study at this suburban junior high school indicates that both the instrument and noninstrument groups made gains, However, the use of instruments produced marked gains in rate with equivalent gains in comprehension not matched by noninstrument groups.

Wilson, Rosemary G. "What's Happening in Philadelphia," *The Reading Teacher,* Vol. 11, No. 3 (February 1958), pp. 185–88.

A "peaceful revolution" in Philadelphia secondary schools—regularly scheduled reading classes even for the gifted.

Bethel Park School District, Pennsylvania.

A team-teaching approach that provides students with an opportunity to work in small groups as well as in large groups in grades four through six.

Centinela Valley Union High School District, California.

Reading laboratory periods are mandatory for eight weeks for all freshman English students. For the rest of the term there are meetings two days a week with a reading specialist.

Walled Lake Junior High School, Michigan.

Reading is taught through a core approach in grades seven through nine.

# GUIDES TO
# PLANNING THE INSTRUCTIONAL PROGRAM

## In the Literature

DeBoer, John, and Dallman, Martha. *The Teaching of Reading* (New York: Holt, Rinehart and Winston, 1960).

Presents current thinking and research on reading; suggests implications of research for classroom practice.

Gans, Roma. *Common Sense in Teaching Reading* (Indianapolis: Bobbs-Merrill Co., 1963).

A book of good, tried and true practices in the teaching of developmental reading.

Harris, Albert. *Effective Teaching of Reading* (New York: David McKay Company, 1962).

Complete treatment of the modern elementary reading program. Contains effective instructional procedures and practices and ample illustrative material.

Kough, J. *Practical Programs for the Gifted* (Chicago: Science Research Associates, 1960).

A how-to-do-it book. Outlines steps in establishing a special program. Based on the opinions and experiences of specialists nominated as experts in the field.

Robinson, F. P. "Study Skills for Superior Students in Secondary Schools," *The Reading Teacher*, Vol. 15, No. 1 (September 1961), pp. 29–33.

Author states that superior students may not be superior readers unless they are given special instruction; one method advocated is SQ3R.

Umans, Shelley. "The Responsibility of the Reading Consultant," *The Reading Teacher*, Vol. 17, No. 1 (September 1963), pp. 16–24.

Suggests an "operating plan" between the reading consultant and the educational community—from the members of the board of education to the professional staff to the community groups.

Weiss, M. Jerry. *Reading in the Secondary School* (New York: Odyssey Press, 1961).

Useful book for secondary school teachers and administrators. Compilation of articles pertinent to teaching reading at high school level.

Zirbes, Laura. *Spurs to Creative Teaching* (New York: G. P. Putnam's Sons, 1959).

Creative approaches in teaching reading (Chapter 8); some good ideas about creative teachers and extensive reading (Chapter 9).

### From the Schools

Madeira, Sheldon. "Pennsylvania's Mandated Reading Program," *Journal of Developmental Reading,* Vol. 5, No. 4 (Summer 1962), pp. 221–26.

Report on the reasons for and acceptance of the compulsory reading program in Pennsylvania. Reports on the reading center in Cheyney College.

Manning, W. R., and Olsen, L. R. "Petaluma Plan for Academically Talented High School Students," *California Journal of Secondary Education,* Vol. 35, No. 8 (December 1960), pp. 510–12.

A tutorial approach to the pursuit of ideas.

Oppenheim, June. "Teaching Reading as a Thinking Process," *The Reading Teacher,* Vol. 13, No. 3 (February 1960), pp. 188–93.

Outlines a primary reading program in use at the Laboratory School of the University of Chicago.

Ramsey, W. "Evaluation of a Joplin Plan of Grouping for Reading Instruction," *Journal of Educational Research,* Vol. 55, No. 10 (August 1962), pp. 567–72.

Author prefers Joplin plan to the self-contained classroom.

## GUIDES TO SELECTING INSTRUCTIONAL MATERIALS

### In the Literature

Brown, James W., and others. *A-V Instruction: Materials and Methods* (New York: McGraw-Hill Book Company, 1959).

Use of certain audio-visual materials (tape recorder, film strips, television, overhead projector) in teaching reading skills and for teaching reading in the content areas.

Burns, P. C. "Booklist to Stimulate Reading in Mentally Advanced Middle-Graders," *The Instructor,* Vol. 71, No. 3 (November 1961), p. 22.

Aid for teacher in selecting books for the developmental reading program.

Graff, P. J. "Materials for Individualized Reading," *Elementary English,* Vol. 38, No. 1 (January 1961), pp. 1–7.

How to assemble necessary materials for individualized reading programs in the primary grades.

Margulies, Stuart, and Lewis D. Eigen. *Programmed Instruction Applied* (New York: John Wiley and Sons, 1962).

Authors offer a penetrating analysis of role of machines in teaching. Answers frequent questions about how much money; how much time; teaching machines or programed books; what situations.

McCreary, R. V. "Meeting Individual Needs," *Elementary English,* Vol. 36, No. 5 (May 1959), pp. 294–97.

Use of differentiated materials to meet all needs of the heterogeneous elementary classroom.

Weiss, M. Jerry. *Reading in the Secondary School* (New York: Odyssey Press, 1961).

Principles for selecting methods and materials to promote growth in reading (Chapter 11). How to develop spontaneity, creativity, critical evaluation, and effective study habits.

### From the Schools

Arcadia, California, Unified School District. *Develop Reading Through Reading Games.* Arcadia Board of Education, 1956.

Alameda, California, Unified School District, *Reading Activities, Grades 1–4.* Alameda Board of Education, 1955–1956.

Dallas, Texas, Independent School District. *Elementary Education, Grades 4, 5, 6* (3 vols.). Dallas Board of Education, 1953.

Madison, Wisconsin, Public Schools. *Word Games.* Madison Board of Education, 1951.

Suggestions for reading activities.

Nashville, Tennessee, Public Schools. *Library Lessons for Intermediate Grades.* Nashville Board of Education, 1956.

# THE REMEDIAL READING PROGRAM

Most youngsters respond well to a developmental program. Others, for a variety of reasons, do not read up to their ability. This presents numerous learning problems and may precipitate social and emotional problems. Students with reading disabilities need corrective help, for as they progress through school the span between achievement and potential grows larger and the prognosis for cure becomes dimmer.

As with the term "developmental," it is difficult to find agreement as to the definition of "remedial." Therefore, in order to provide a frame of reference, let us use the following definition: A *remedial program* is for those students who, because of a reading disability, are not achieving up to their potential as it is measured by ability tests, by their teachers' estimates of their potential, or even by their own appraisal. Some of these students may be reading "on grade level" but, because of their intellectual ability, should be reading several years "above grade level." It is inaccurate to judge retardation solely by the student's age and grade placement.

Remedial reading should not be confused with reading clinic services. A reading clinic is designed for students who are severely retarded in reading and, in addition, have psychological and physiological problems. Because of the complexity of these problems, remedial programs, as defined here, do not apply to these children, for they require a clinical approach. (For a brief description of a clinic program see pages 61–63.)

Although the remedial reading teacher has the primary responsibility for the remedial program, every teacher and supervisor shares this responsibility because the periods in a remedial reading room are few, and the largest portion of a student's time is spent in the regular classroom. Therefore, in setting up a remedial reading program, the reading teacher should plan the program with the other members of the teaching staff.

## CRITERIA FOR SELECTION OF PUPILS

The selection of pupils for the remedial program should be based on realistic standards. Ideally, it would be advisable to include students who have only slight reading disabilities, since many of these students can be brought up to their reading potential in a short time. However, a school in which there is only one remedial reading teacher and three hundred students need help in reading cannot assign students with a slight retardation to remedial classes. The usual practice is to take those students who need the most help and who the teacher feels will respond to the remedial program.

In setting up remedial classes, it is important to set criteria for admission. Such criteria will change, of course, with the number of students in need of help and the available facilities. The following criteria are offered as a guide line, not as a "formula."

### Mental Ability and Reading Retardation

The prognosis for improvement in reading is, of course, more favorable when the student has average (or higher than average) mental ability. Children with below normal ability often benefit from a remedial reading program, but their improvement will not be as rapid as that of children with normal ability. The decision whether or not to accept students of below normal ability must be determined before embarking on a program.

In order to determine mental ability, one should examine the IQ score. That score, however, should not necessarily be accepted at face value. For example, if the student's score was obtained with a group test requiring reading skills beyond the student's achievement, he would not be able to read the questions and answer intelligently. His lack of reading ability will depress the score and give a meaningless or damaging impression of his mental ability.

In studying a student's testing record, it is important to note the test scores of all intelligence tests administered to him to determine if the pattern is constant or if the results vary. For example, if a group test shows an IQ of 105 in the first grade, 95 in the third grade, and 85 in the sixth grade, one might inquire further into the reason for these varying IQ scores. A first-grade IQ score is based on a nonverbal test. Since subsequent test scores, in this example, indicate an IQ drop of 20 points, it is possible that this drop may have been caused by the student's inability to read the test items. In such cases, individual intelligence tests, such as the WISC or the Stanford-Binet, should be administered by a school psychologist. These instruments do not necessarily require reading ability to indicate intelligence.

In addition, there is considerable evidence that the present verbal intelligence tests work to the disadvantage of those whose backgrounds are not comparable to the tests' normative population. This is particularly true in the case of students with limited economic, educational, and cultural backgrounds. Since these students must function in the environment in which the test was normed, however alien it might be to them, the prognosis for achievement in the environment is poor. A concomitant program of cultural enrichment should be offered with the remedial reading instruction.

Once a student's mental ability has been determined, the next step is to measure the discrepancy between his potential and his present reading ability. This can be done by first finding his "mental age." The mental age is arrived at by multiplying the IQ by the chronological age and then dividing the result by 100. For example, an IQ of 140 and a chronological age (CA) of 10 years equals a mental age (MA) of 14. (Tables for converting raw scores to reading age—RA—are provided in most reading-test manuals.) In order to determine the difference between the MA and the RA, the RA is subtracted from the MA. For example:

$$\text{IQ } 140 \times \text{CA } 10 = \frac{1400}{100} = \text{MA } 14$$

MA 14.0 − RA 10.4 = 3.6 reading retardation

### School Placement

Priority for remedial reading instruction should be given to those students who show reading disability at an early age. The third grade in the elementary school is the crucial time to identify those pupils who are beginning to fall behind in reading. (There are those, however, who believe that the end of the first year of school is the critical time.) If these youngsters are not given help at an early stage, the gap between their chronological age and their ability to read will widen as they grow older. If a third-grade student is one year below grade level in reading, it is possible that unless corrective measures are taken he will be four years below grade level when he reaches the eighth grade. It is easier to help students if their reading disabilities are identified early in the school career. This is not to say that all third-grade students who are reading only one year below grade placement have reading disabilities. At this early stage in a child's development, a score of one year below grade level may be caused by physical or emotional immaturity and would not necessarily be indicative of a reading disability. This youngster should, however, be watched because if the discrepancy continues it may result in a reading disability. A wise teacher should be able to determine whether or not remedial reading is appropriate at this time.

Reading disabilities may occur at almost any time in a student's school experience; they may arise in the fifth, sixth, or seventh grades, or even in the upper high school grades as well as in the early grades. If the classroom teacher discovers these late developing deficiencies, remedial measures should be taken immediately. For this reason, a careful study of reading ability should be undertaken in the middle grades and in the early junior high school grades.

### Attitude toward Reading Instruction

By means of an interview with a student, the remedial reading teacher may discover the student's general attitude toward learning and his specific attitude toward attending a remedial reading class. Remedial reading programs are usually overcrowded. Therefore, unless a student has a positive attitude toward the program, it is usually not wise to include him.

The remedial reading teacher should thoroughly investigate the reasons a student has been referred to the program. Many of these students may be discipline problems in the regular classroom. Nevertheless, the remedial reading teacher may decide to include some of these students if they demonstrate a positive attitude toward the corrective help. In an initial classroom session with such students, the remedial reading teacher should establish rules for classroom conduct and control.

In the course of the term, if a student continues to present control problems, the remedial reading teacher should then seek assistance from members of the guidance team and, if necessary, have the students removed from the program.

## DETERMINING READING ACHIEVEMENT

After deciding which students are to be accepted in the program, the next step is to analyze the students' needs and abilities.

As with the developmental program, we would first want a general idea of where the youngster is reading. Is he very much behind grade level? Is his reading ability trailing behind his mental age? In what large general areas is he deficient: word recognition, reading comprehension, rate of reading? This information may be gained from a standardized test. However, a degree of caution must be exercised here. Poor readers tend to "guess" on standardized tests and so test marks often tend to overestimate the level at which the child can actually read.

A more reliable source of determining reading achievement of poor readers is a diagnostic test such as the Gates–McKillop, Munroe, or Durrell diagnostic tests. Any of these tests have value in as much as they divide the reading process into sets of skills and they test each skill. However, one must remember that reading is not made up of discrete skills, each unrelated to the others. It is, in fact, a syndrome of skills, with each affecting the others. Therefore, the results of a diagnostic test that explores separate skills must be taken cautiously. A test score is not diagnostic; it is merely an indication to a teacher to "look further."

Emmet Betts[1] separates achievement into three levels: *basal level*, the highest readability level at which the individual can read by himself without symptoms of frustration; *instructional level*, the highest level at which the learner can read satisfactorily under teacher supervision in a group situation; *frustration level*,

[1] Emmet Betts, "Informal Inventories," in *Handbook of Corrective Reading for the American Adventure Series* (New York: Harper and Brothers, 1952).

the level at which symptoms of frustration set in, such as finger pointing, tension movements, a high-pitched voice.

The best way to determine these "achievement levels" is through the informal inventory. These informal tests or graded inventories are described in the preceding chapter on developmental reading. Desirable for use with the normal reader, they are practically a requirement for the remedial student.

Diagnosis, however, should include more than test scores or skills deficiencies. It must include how the youngster feels toward reading. Is he afraid to read; does he "hate" reading; does he use the lack of reading ability as a weapon? Any of these attitudes will affect your ability to help him.  •

Determining the reading achievement of students with reading disabilities is a tricky and difficult business. Too often, we are tempted to take results of diagnostic instruments as gospel. A remedial program, properly planned, must take into consideration the fact that diagnosis rests primarily with the teacher, using whatever test results he may feel have value but primarily using a common sense problem solving approach to the study of children with reading difficulties.

## SELECTING PATTERNS OF ORGANIZATION

Now let us assume that those students who need remedial help have been identified. The decision will then have to be made as to the most effective way of reaching these students. The appropriate program will be determined to a large extent by the number of students who need help, the number of remedial reading teachers provided by the school, and the amount of classroom teacher involvement desired. For example, if 300 students need remedial reading and only one remedial reading position is provided for, it will be impossible for the remedial reading teacher to meet all the youngsters. That school would require a plan that would either service only one segment of the students needing help or combine the remedial reading program and the classroom program. Whichever plan is chosen, it should be kept in mind that although the special reading teacher has the primary responsibility for this program, every teacher and supervisor on the professional staff shares in the responsibility. Therefore, in setting up the remedial reading program, the reading teacher, the school supervisor, and the classroom teacher should confer and plan the program cooperatively.

In considering any of these plans, it is important to understand that an organizational structure should be the result of educational needs, not a set structure in which to place students. Every plan has advantages and disadvantages, and only with careful study and the spirit of testing by trial and error can an appropriate plan be selected.

### The Conventional Plan

In many schools that have remedial reading programs, the students come from many different classrooms and meet for a common period of reading instruction. The students in the corrective classes may be classified or grouped in a number of ways: according to reading achievement, grade placement, reading disabilities, or reading interests. Important to organizing for instruction, grouping does not insure successful learning. It is the content of the lesson that directs learning. Grouping for instruction should not prevent us from offering a balanced program of instruction. Although a student may need intensive help in one area, other areas must not be neglected. Grouping procedures that "freeze" in one skill area to the exclusion of the others cannot produce a competent reader.

A balanced program of instruction, implemented by "flexible grouping," should emphasize those areas of skill building that develop meaningful vocabulary; teach word recognition skills; improve comprehension; and develop study skills. Reading instruction should be integrated with teaching of content, and at the same time should develop an interest in literature.

Most schools try to set up the program so that the student goes to his remedial reading class at the same time the rest of his class is receiving reading instruction. Even so, this plan has drawbacks because the student misses the lesson covered in the classroom. But it is even worse to schedule corrective reading in conflict with other subjects. When this is done, the students miss the work covered in the subject class while they are in corrective reading, and no matter how well they do in the special reading class, they may not be able to make up what they have missed.

This plan makes little or no provision for cooperative planning between the remedial reading teacher and the classroom teacher. It would be impossible for the reading teacher to parallel the content from all the classrooms from which the students come. What is more, the classroom teacher is unaware of what his students are doing in the reading room. Because of this, little provision is made for continuing corrective practices in the classroom, and the skill of corrective teaching remains solely with the special reading teacher.

There are other approaches to organization for remedial reading classes that some schools have found more effective. Each has certain merits but no one approach is recommended over another. What is effective in one school may be completely unsuitable for another.

### Cooperative Planning

In this organization the classroom teacher (English teacher in the secondary school) shares the remedial reading program with the special reading teacher. During part of the time set aside for English instruction, the class is divided into two parts for reading instruction. The special reading teacher works with that half of the class most in need of corrective instruction in one room and, in another room, the classroom teacher works with the other half of the class teaching those reading skills that are needed by that group. Together, both teachers plan the lessons so that the two groups receive comparable instruction as to content. At mid-year the groups are exchanged, and the two teachers continue to plan together. One of the advantages of the program is that all students are given the opportunity to work with the reading specialist. Another is that the classroom teacher is given the opportunity of learning how to build a remedial reading program through cooperative planning with a reading teacher.

For this plan to work effectively, the classroom teacher and the remedial reading teacher must have time assigned during the school day to meet to plan instruction. If this is not possible, the plan is impractical.

### The Reading Teacher as an Assistant
### to the Classroom Teacher

In this plan the reading teacher plans the lessons for those students requiring remedial reading and the lessons are given in the regular classroom. The reading teacher works with this group at the same time as the classroom teacher proceeds with his lesson. The lessons are built around the same content that the classroom teacher presents to the major part of the class, but the reading skills are taught through less demanding materials. Then, after the classroom teacher has assigned his students an application activity on the lesson that was taught, he observes the reading teacher working with the smaller remedial group. This affords the classroom teacher the opportunity of learning, from the specialist, methods of remedial reading instruction, while the students as they receive help in reading are able to keep abreast of their classmates. After several months (depending on the abilities of the teacher), the reading teacher leaves the classroom, and the regular teacher assumes the responsibility for the corrective instruction with the small group.

This plan, of course, has obvious limitations. Both the reading teacher and the classroom teacher have to be skilled in paralleling instruction on different levels. This is a task made even more difficult when there is a lack of instructional materials that provide for similar content on different reading levels. In addition, the time spent by the students in "quiet work" while the classroom teacher is observing the remedial reading lesson must not degenerate to "busy work." It must be meaningful and appropriate. This calls for highly skilled planning. Then, too, not all teachers feel comfortable in a teaching situation when a colleague is in the same room.

However, this plan has been introduced in Philadelphia and has been used experimentally by a number of school systems throughout the country. It is a practical method of demonstration teaching in a natural setting. A more detailed discussion of this type of organization appeared in an article in *The Reading Teacher*.[2]

## The Reading Teacher as an Auxiliary Teacher

In this arrangement the classroom teacher and the reading specialist jointly plan all the reading lessons for the week. Together they formulate lesson objectives, teaching procedures, and application activities. The first lesson each week is given as a demonstration lesson by the reading teacher with the classroom

[2] Shelley Umans, "A New Type of Remedial Reading Program in the Junior High School," *The Reading Teacher*, Vol. 4 (April 1957), p. 215.

teacher observing. The lesson is designed to motivate and prepare the class for the instruction that will follow. After this initial lesson, the classroom teacher, on his own, gives the lessons for the remainder of the week.

This organization offers the classroom teacher the opportunity of planning reading lessons under the guidance of a reading specialist, yet allows for the individual teacher's initiative and imagination. It also makes it possible for the reading specialist to work with a large number of teachers and students. As many as ten teachers can participate in this program if the reading specialist is scheduled to teach two classes each day. The remainder of the day may be spent in conferences with teachers for planning the week's lessons, in preparation of materials to be used in the demonstration, and in consultation with supervisors and administrators.

The remedial reading teacher has little personal contact with students. His talents are diffused and spread out over large numbers of both students and teachers. The results are less dramatic than either of the two previously presented plans. However, from a long-range point of view, the dividends may be greater, since many of the classroom teachers who have worked with the remedial teacher may eventually become more competent in the teaching of reading, thus affecting many more students.

### The Reading Teacher Acts as a "Core" Teacher

In this plan students with severe reading disabilities meet with the reading teacher for a part of each day. Reading becomes the core through which all subjects are taught. The specialist becomes the content teacher and scales the curriculum to the reading ability of these students. For example, the reading specialist meets the students for a block of periods in which he teaches English, social studies, mathematics, and science. He teaches reading skills through using the content of each of these subjects. This approach should not consume all periods in a school day. The students should join their homeroom group for art, music, health and physical education, industrial arts, and for any other subjects not covered in the "core" program.

Although this organization has the advantage of offering students a rich and concentrated remedial program, it has the disadvantage of earmarking a segment of the school population as being different and needing special help. It has the additional disadvantage of limiting the number of students with whom the reading teacher may work. As few as twenty students in an entire school year may be serviced by the reading teacher, which makes this a fairly expensive program.

## PLANNING THE INSTRUCTIONAL PROGRAM

In planning a remedial reading program one should gather as much information as possible about the individual student. By the time the student is accepted in the remedial reading program, the reading teacher should have some indication of his mental ability, a clue to the extent of his reading retardation, and some idea as to his specific disabilities. This is a start, but there is much more to learn if we hope to provide effective help.

### The Cumulative Record Card

By examining a student's cumulative record card, teachers may be alerted to some of the following significant information:

1. *Mobility.* A student who has moved from one section of the country to another or from one part of the city to another may have encountered numerous approaches to the teaching of reading. This diversity often affects reading achievement.
2. *Language spoken in the home.* When a foreign language is spoken at home (to the exclusion of English), it is difficult for a student to practice his new language. This may have a direct bearing on a student's reading patterns.
3. *Child's position in the family.* Sometimes the child's position in the family suggests ways in which he is treated by other members of the family; the youngest may have problems or responsibilities different from the middle or eldest child. These problems or responsibilities may have an effect on the child's self concept and, in turn, on his learning.
4. *Attendance records.* A student who is absent for long periods of time or at frequent intervals suffers from interruptions in the continuity of his school program. Since reading is taught in sequential steps, these interruptions present serious obstacles to his reading progress. In studying the attendance record, a teacher may note that a student had a prolonged absence in the fourth grade. It may have been at this time that a

reading disability set in and, on checking the test record, the teacher may find that the test score has remained on the fourth-grade level. This may be a valuable clue and may indicate that instruction should be initiated on that level.

5. *Health record.* The teacher should note physical factors, such as visual and aural difficulties, or psychological handicaps that might influence a student's reading ability. Health records should be studied in conjunction with attendance records.

6. *Special agency referrals.* If agency referrals are indicated on a record, the teacher may wish to confer with the guidance counselor to see if reports appropriate to reading problems are available.

7. *Test record.* A student's cumulative record should be studied for indications of patterns of performance.

8. *Achievement records.* The teacher should examine the grades given in each subject area to see if they indicate achievement patterns which would provide clues to the student's reading ability. Higher grades in mathematics and science than in English and history might indicate a reading problem, since both English and history are "reading subjects." Outstanding achievement in industrial arts or health education gives the remedial reading teacher a clue to the student's interests. The content of these subjects might be highly motivating materials for corrective instruction. Achievement records should be studied with attendance records and health records. A drop in school grades may have come at the same time as a prolonged absence and a serious illness.

9. *Anecdotal records.* Anecdotal comments are most helpful when they describe specific qualities and suggest effective methods of instruction for a particular student. Some school systems include records or reports of parent-teacher conferences which might also be helpful in guiding the remedial reading teacher. Comments by teachers may be helpful as supplementary information, but they may also reveal inaccurate and subjective judgments which could be damaging to the student.

### The Reading Profile

After as much information as possible has been culled from the student's record card, the remedial reading teacher should want a record of all other activities related to the student's reading status. This record should become part of the student's guidance folder so that it can be consulted throughout his school career and particularly during the period in which he is in the remedial reading program. The profile would include information relevant to his admission to the program: test records, general interests, hobbies, career interests, attitudes toward reading, health data, observations on his personality, and that part of his family history which is pertinent to his reading problems. It should also include a record of his school attendance, his achievement in his subject areas, and a specific analysis of his reading skills. Careful attention should be given to this last section since the analysis indicates which skills need corrective work. A complete profile would also include a description of the corrective program: textbooks, trade books, teacher-made materials, and procedures used with the student. There are many types of reading records. Each teacher must decide how much and what type of material is useful. On the basis of the reading profile, the remedial reading teacher can begin to form groups within whatever pattern of organization is decided upon.

An example of a reading profile that can be used by the remedial reading teacher in either an elementary or a secondary school appears on the following pages. With the information on the profile, assembled from the cumulative record card, tests, and interviews, the teacher is ready to proceed with his program. The "how to," or methods, of teaching remedial reading are not discussed in this book. To do so would be to repeat what has already been said often and well by reading experts.

## READING PROFILE

*General Data*

Name of Pupil _____ Address _____

Grade _____ Sex _____ Date of Birth _____

Place of Birth _____ Number of Years in School System _____

Source of Referral:
    Record Cards _____ Teacher _____ Pupil _____ Other _____

Date Admitted to Reading Group _____ Date Dismissed _____

Reason for Dismissal:
    Reading Age up to Mental Age _____ Up to School Grade _____

    Transferred to _____ Other Reasons _____

*Test Record*

    (Enter results of group tests, and of individual tests if available)

## READING PROFILE (Continued)

INTELLIGENCE

| NAME | FORM | DATE | IQ | COMMENTS |
|------|------|------|-----|----------|
|      |      |      |     |          |
|      |      |      |     |          |
|      |      |      |     |          |

READING

| NAME | FORM | DATE | READING GRADE | COMMENTS |
|------|------|------|---------------|----------|
|      |      |      |               |          |
|      |      |      |               |          |
|      |      |      |               |          |
|      |      |      |               |          |
|      |      |      |               |          |

*General Interests*

A. Hobbies and Outstanding Interests _____

_____

_____

B. Career Interests _____

_____

C. Attitude toward
   Reading _____

_____

_____

   Remedial Group _____

_____

_____

*Health Data*

|                         | BE SPECIFIC | REMEDIAL MEASURES |
|-------------------------|-------------|-------------------|
| Vision _____ |             |                   |
| Hearing _____ |             |                   |
| Speech _____ |             |                   |
| General Health _____ |             |                   |
| Serious Illness or Injury ___ |       |                   |

*Personality*

|                         | CHECK | COMMENTS |
|-------------------------|-------|----------|
| A. Behavior             |       |          |
| Dependent _____   |       |          |
| Docile, Shy _____  |       |          |
| Seeks Attention _____  |       |          |
| Moody _____    |       |          |
| Overconfident _____  |       |          |
| Aggressive _____   |       |          |

## READING PROFILE (Continued)

B. Outstanding Problems _____

_____

_____

C. Referrals

    Agency _____ Date _____ Under Treatment? _____

    _____ _____ _____

D. Confidential File Exists in School     Yes _____ No _____

*Family History*

Are Both Parents Living at Home? _____

Number of Children in Family _____

Languages Spoken in the Home _____

Treatment of Child by Parents _____

Parents' Cooperation with School _____

*School History*

| Attendance | ELEM. SCHOOL | J. H. SCHOOL | CORRECTIVE RDG. GROUP |
|---|---|---|---|
| Excellent | _____ | _____ | _____ |
| Good | _____ | _____ | _____ |
| Poor | _____ | _____ | _____ |

Grade Progress:

    Normal _____ Held Over _____ Accelerated _____

School Subjects:

| DOES WELL IN | NEEDS HELP IN |
|---|---|
| _____ | _____ |
| _____ | _____ |
| _____ | _____ |
| _____ | _____ |

*Contact with Subject Teacher*

| DATE | REMARKS |
|---|---|
| _____ | _____ |
| _____ | _____ |
| _____ | _____ |
| _____ | _____ |
| _____ | _____ |
| _____ | _____ |

*Comments and Anecdotal Records:*

Date of Summary _____ Made by _____

## READING PROFILE (Continued)

*Reading Check List*

INDICATE DATE CHECKED

SILENT READING
  Pointing _____
  Vocalization _____
  Rate _____
  Regressions _____
COMPREHENSION
  Lacks Ability to:
    Understand concepts _____
    Understand general
      significance _____
    Remember important detail _____
    Follow directions _____
    Draw conclusions _____
ORAL READING
  Word by word reading _____
  Pointing _____
  Substitution _____
  Reversals _____
  Omissions _____
  Insertions _____
WORD RECOGNITION
  Fails to use:
    Configuration clues _____
    Context clues _____
  Structural analysis _____
  Phonic analysis _____
    Ability to analyze and blend _____
    Knowledge of letter names _____
    Knowledge of letter sounds _____
SPECIAL STUDY SKILLS
  Lacks ability to use:
    Maps, globes _____
    Parts of a book—index,
      contents _____
    Dictionary, encyclopedias _____

*Pupil's Diagnosis of His Own Reading Difficulty*

_____

_____

*Description of Instructional Program*

A. Materials used in reading program
     Devices _____
     Basal Reader (if any) _____
     Types of Books interested in _____

### READING PROFILE (Continued)

B. Procedures in remedial instruction (include changes made as work
   progresses) _____

_____

_____

Note: Some of the information on the profile can be gained only after a
period of time during which the teacher gains insight into the pupil's
background; hence, considerable time may elapse before the completion
of the profile.

## SELECTING INSTRUCTIONAL MATERIALS

Instructional materials for students with reading disabilities
are numerous. There was a time when little was available and
teachers had to create their own materials. Publishers, now
aware of the large numbers of students in the "below grade
level" group, are prolific in meeting the demands. The major
problem is no longer how to get materials but rather to determine whether the materials are appropriate for the particular
student.

We are well aware of the need for highly motivating reading
material for those who have reading disabilities. However, a
single publisher cannot decide what would be interesting content
to all youngsters. Therefore, it becomes the responsibility of the
remedial reading teacher to be highly selective in the materials
he chooses. The following are some guides to selecting materials:

1. Is the format of the book appropriate to the grade level of
   the student who will be using the book? (For example, a large
   picture-type paperbound book is often offensive to the seventh
   grader who wants to read a book that looks like "all other
   seventh-grade books.")
2. Is the content of the book meaningful and realistic, or does
   it presuppose cultural experience that the child may not have
   had?
3. Does the content complement the curriculum; will it be meaningful to the student in his classroom work?
4. Is the size of the print appropriate to the reading ability of
   the student?
5. Are the illustrations interesting and helpful in getting meanings of words and concepts?
6. Is the vocabulary sufficiently challenging and interesting so
   that words encourage thinking?

7. Is the book well organized so that the student can easily locate material?
8. Is the content timely and accurate?
9. Does the book have commendable literary qualities?

Most of these guides are important for all students, whether or not they have reading disabilities, but they are particularly important for the youngster who is "in trouble," since the book that he reads is his final measure of achievement.

In addition to books, there are periodicals, practice materials, audio-visual aids such as films, filmstrips, and records, and reading instruments such as tachistoscopes, reading pacers, overhead projectors, and teaching machines. Again, all of these must be evaluated as to their appropriateness to the individual student.

Materials are an important adjunct to teaching. They should be attractively displayed, made easily accessible, and kept in good condition. Book publishers are cooperative in supplying schools with samples of current materials, but the final selection and ordering of instructional materials should be in the hands of the teacher.

## GUIDES TO
## DETERMINING READING ACHIEVEMENT

### In the Literature

Austin, M. C., Bush, C. L., and Huebner, M. H. *Reading Evaluation* (New York: Ronald Press, 1961), pp. 10–11.

> An inventory of skills from grade one through grade eight (based on Sheldon Basal Readers). This inventory may be used with other materials.

Betts, Emmet Albert. "Informal Inventories." In *Handbook on Corrective Reading for the American Adventure Series* (New York: Harper and Brothers, 1952), pp. 3–8.

> Methods for teachers of creating informal inventories for groups and individuals.

Kough, Jack, and DeHaan, Robert. *Identifying Children with Special Needs* (Chicago: Science Research Associates, 1955).

> Informal methods of determining special reading disabilities.

Plessas, Gus, and Ludley, D. M. "Spelling Ability and Poor Reading," *Elementary School Journal*, Vol. 63, No. 7 (April 1963), pp. 404–08.

How the Gilmore Oral Reading Test was used to assess reading growth in an experiment in the Sacramento area with 58 boys and 15 girls, ranging in age from eight to sixteen years.

Smith, Nila Banton. *Graded Selections for Informal Reading* (New York: New York University Press, 1959).

An inventory for grades one through three. Interesting selections, clearl; graded.

## Tests

Durrell, Donald D. *Durrell Analysis of Reading Difficulty* (New York: World Book Company, 1955).

Focuses on a checklist of errors on which there are no normative data but on which remediation can be based.

Gates, Arthur I., and McKillop, Anne S. *Reading Diagnostic Tests* (New York: Bureau of Publications, Teachers College, Columbia University, 1962).

Detailed diagnosis of reading ability for elementary school pupils.

Madden, M., and Pratt, M. "An Oral Reading Survey as a Teaching Aid," *Elementary English Review,* Vol. 18, No. 4 (April 1941), pp. 122–26.

Subject content of test is mainly social studies and science.

Monroe, Marion. *Monroe Diagnostic Reading Examination* (Chicago: C. H. Stollting Company).

Focuses remedial attention on oral reading errors occurring with greater frequency than in a specified norm group.

# GUIDES TO
# SELECTING PATTERNS OF ORGANIZATION

## In the Literature

Amidon, Edmund, and Flanders, Ned. "Self Directed Group Work in the Elementary Schools," *Elementary English,* Vol. 40, No. 4 (April 1963), pp. 373–78.

A description of a self directed group in which the teacher is not the leader but acts as a guide or resource person.

Hull, C. M. "Levels Program for Junior High School," *Elementary Education,* Vol. 50 (March 1962), pp. 295–96.

The grouping of students according to their abilities rather than by grades is described.

Lanning, Frank W. "Dyadic Reading," *Elementary English*, Vol. 39, No. 3 (March 1962), pp. 244–45.

A one-to-one relationship of two students—each chosen with a specific ability in order to help each other.

Rothrock, Dayton M. "Heterogeneous–Homogeneous or Individual Approach to Reading?" *Elementary English*, Vol. 38, No. 4 (April 1961), pp. 233–38.

Each approach is described with its merits and limitations.

Shane, Harold. "Grouping in the Elementary School," *Phi Delta Kappan*, Vol. 41, No. 7 (April 1960), pp. 313–18.

Several possible and new methods of grouping.

Sheldon, William. "Reading Instruction in the Junior High Schools." In *Citizenship and a Free Society: Education for the Future*. 30th Yearbook of the National Council for the Social Studies (Washington, D.C.: National Education Association, 1960), pp. 305–19.

A description of how subject area classes are used for reading instruction periods.

### From the Schools

Ector County Independent School District, Odessa, Texas.

Strong basal reading program combined with a large library circulation.

Heathcote Elementary School, Scarsdale, New York.

All students attend a reading laboratory that provides them with skills instruction in the various subject disciplines. (Remedial and developmental.)

Lichtenstein, J. "New Castle Reading Experiment in Cleveland Heights," *Elementary English*, Vol. 37, No. 1 (January 1960), pp. 27–28.

How Cleveland Heights successfully used the New Castle experiment.

Morgan, E. F., Sr., and Stuckler, G. R. "Joplin Plan of Reading Verses: A Traditional Method," *Journal of Educational Psychology*, Vol. 51, No. 2 (April 1960), pp. 69–73.

Findings seem to indicate that teaching or, more probably, learning effectiveness increases as the group becomes more truly homogeneous.

Nicolet High School, Milwaukee, Wisconsin.

A highly structured program that introduces a "skill a month" in the various subject disciplines.

Pennsylvania Department of Education, Harrisburg, Pennsylvania.

An outline of a mandated program by the state for instruction in reading in the secondary schools. (Remedial and developmental.)

St. Louis, Missouri, Public Schools.

Concentrated instruction in fundamentals for small groups not ready to enter the fourth grade in elementary schools.

Umans, Shelley. *New Trends in Reading Instruction* (New York: Bureau of Publications, Teachers College, Columbia University, 1963).

Many new approaches to grouping in the self-contained classroom and in the subject-matter classroom are discussed.

# GUIDES TO
# PLANNING THE INSTRUCTIONAL PROGRAM

## In the Literature

Heilman, Arthur W. *Phonics in Proper Perspective* (Columbus, Ohio: Charles E. Merrill Co., 1964).

A "how and why" book in the teaching of phonics.

Johnson, Marjorie Sheldon. "Reading Instruction in the Clinic," *The Reading Teacher,* Vol. 15, No. 6 (May 1962), pp. 415–20.

Techniques peculiar to a reading clinic are outlined and briefly described.

Robinson, H. Alan. "A Cluster of Skills: Especially for Junior High School," *The Reading Teacher,* Vol. 15, No. 1 (September 1961), pp. 25–28.

Plea for the junior high school teacher to consider study skills in clusters of small units ("key thought" clusters): key words in a sentence (Step 1); key sentences in a paragraph (Step 2); key thought in a paragraph (Step 3).

Robinson, Helen, and Smith, Helen. "Rate Problems in the Reading Clinic," *The Reading Teacher,* Vol. 15, No. 6 (May 1962), pp. 421–26.

Some new methods to help pupils with reading disabilities improve their rate of reading.

Winston, Gertrude. "Oral Reading and Group Reading," *Elementary English,* Vol. 40, No. 4 (April 1963), pp. 392–94.

A description of activities that a teacher can use in making oral reading interesting to children.

From the Schools

Thomas A. Edison High School, Philadelphia, Pennsylvania.

An imaginative approach to ungrading two aspects of the English language arts: reading comprehension and English usage.

Olsen, Arthur. "Phonics and Success in Beginning Reading," *Journal of Developmental Reading*, Vol. 6, No. 4 (Summer 1963), pp. 256–60.

Study carried on with large groups of first-grade youngsters in the Boston area seems to indicate that requiring a child to develop a 75-word sight vocabulary is unjustified; rather, a knowledge of the relationships between sounds and letters is essential to development of basic sight vocabulary.

# GUIDES TO
# SELECTING INSTRUCTIONAL MATERIALS

In the Literature

Bloomfield, L., and Barnhart, C. L. *Let's Read: A Linguistic Approach* (Detroit: Wayne State University Press, 1961).

A combination of a teacher's manual and lessons for students in a basic linguistic approach to beginning and remedial reading.

Downing, J. A. *To Be or Not to Be* (London: Cassell, 1962).

The Augmented Roman Alphabet is illustrated and examples of its use are given. Beginning and remedial reading.

Fry, Edward B. "Teaching Machines and Reading Instruction," *The Reading Teacher*, Vol. 15, No. 1 (September 1961), pp. 43–45.

The possible uses of teaching machines for reading improvement.

Gates, Arthur I. "Teaching Machines in Perspective," *Elementary School Journal*, Vol. 62, No. 1 (October 1961), pp. 1–13.

An overview of the theory and practice of programed instruction.

McDavid, R. T. "The Role of the Linguist in the Teaching of Reading," *Proceedings*, International Reading Association, 1961, pp. 253–56.

Provides a rationale for teaching reading through the structure of the language.

## From the Schools

Iowa State Education Association. *Instructional Games* (Des Moines: The Association, 1959).

Omaha, Nebraska, Public Schools. *A Library Program for Elementary Schools: Reading Activities for Non-Reading Groups in the Elementary Grades.* Omaha Board of Education, 1951.

San Diego County, California, Schools. *A Handbook of Independent Activities.* San Diego County Board of Education, 1959.

Wisconsin State Reading Circle. *Wisconsin Reading Circles.* Madison, Wisconsin, State Department of Public Instruction, published annually.

## READING CLINIC PROGRAM

A reading clinic program is designed for those students who are severely retarded in reading and who, in addition, have other major psychological problems. Clinics should have at their disposal not only reading therapists but psychologists, psychiatrists, and social workers as well. The student should be carefully selected on the basis of intelligence potential, reading ability, and a prognosis which would indicate that clinical help might be effective.

The most common type of reading clinic is the one sponsored by colleges and universities. Primarily, the purpose of these clinics is to provide internship for the graduate student who, under the direct supervision of the university faculty, is learning how to work with students with severe reading disabilities. The number of graduate students in training determines the number of reading clients accepted in the college or university clinic. College and university clinics usually charge low fees and are partially self-supporting. A listing of more than 120 college and university clinics, together with pertinent information available, was published in 1960.[1]

Another type of reading clinic is sponsored by civic or charitable organizations. Examples of these are the Northside Center for Child Development in New York City and the Junior League Reading Center in Chattanooga, Tennessee. Such clinics are usually independent units supported by foundation grants, with very little income from fees.

There are, of course, numerous private reading clinics not

[1] "Directory of Reading Clinics," *EDL Research and Information Bulletin No. 4* (Huntington, New York: Educational Development Laboratories, 1960).

associated with schools or charitable organizations and most often not subject to government supervision. Some of these clinics are directed by people with expert professional preparation and provide a service of extremely high quality. Others, unfortunately, fall short of professional expectations and standards.

Reading clinics organized within public school systems are a fairly recent innovation. One of the first to introduce reading clinics was St. Louis, Missouri, where five centers or clinics are in operation. Each clinic services a group of neighborhood public schools. The staff of the clinic includes a reading specialist, a psychologist, a social worker, and a technician. The reading teachers are elementary school teachers who are assigned to the clinic for a six-month period. They are trained and guided by the reading specialist. At the end to the six-month period, these teachers, now trained in remedial techniques, return to their regular classrooms, and six other teachers join the staff of the reading clinic. This plan has been adopted by the Duluth, Minnesota, school system and, at this point, all the elementary school teachers there have received training in the reading clinic.

In both communities pupils with severe reading disabilities are assigned to the clinics for from two to five instructional periods per week depending upon their need. The student usually receives individual instruction until his word perception skills are developed to the point where he can recognize words independently. At this time he may be given small-group instruction. Pupils remain at the clinics until they can perform independently with the books in use in their regular classrooms. The St. Louis reading clinics in particular are an outstanding example of special reading services supported solely by the school system.

New York City established its first elementary school reading clinic in 1955 and now has nine units. Each unit has a staff of three reading counselors, a full-time psychologist, a full-time psychiatric social worker, a part-time psychiatrist, and a clerk. Descriptions of this program have appeared in reading periodicals.[2] Students are recommended to the clinics by the principals

---

[2] See, for example, Stella S. Cohn, "The Special Reading Services of the New York City Board of Education, Part I: An Overview of the Program," *The Reading Teacher*, Vol. 12, No. 2 (December 1958), pp. 107-14; Margaretta W. Fite and Margaret M. Mosher, "The Special Reading Services of the New York City Board of Education, Part II: The Clinical Program," *The Reading Teacher*, Vol. 12, No. 3 (February 1959), pp. 181–86.

and the guidance counselors in the elementary schools. If accepted in the clinic, the students remain there until they are capable of transferring to a schoolroom setting under the direction of a special reading teacher.

School systems operate generally on limited budgets, and a clinic can be prohibitive in cost. Very often these reading cases are social as well as educational problems, and for this reason, as well as because of budget limitations, the responsibility for the operation of such clinics would properly seem to rest with the community as well as the school system.

## GUIDES TO A READING CLINIC PROGRAM

### In the Literature

Chall, Jeanne S. "Reading Disability and the Role of the Teacher," *Elementary English,* Vol. 35, No. 5 (May 1958), pp. 297–98.

The importance of teaching the student with emotional problems how to read.

Gates, Arthur I. "What We Know and Can Do About the Poor Reader," *Education,* Vol. 77, No. 9 (May 1957), pp. 528–33.

The role of emotional factors, lack of reading skills, and parents' concerns in the development of the retarded reader.

Harris, Albert J. "A Critical Reaction to *The Nature of Reading Disability*," *Journal of Developmental Reading,* Vol. 3, No. 4 (Summer 1960), pp. 238–49.

An analysis of the possible causes of reading disability.

Roswell, Florence, and Natchez, Gladys. *Reading Disabilities* (New York: Basic Books, 1964).

This book examines the complex causes of reading disability and suggests practical methods of diagnosis and treatment.

Smith, D. E. P., and Carrigan, Patricia. *The Nature of Reading Disability* (New York: Harcourt, Brace and Co., 1959).

A physiological approach to the causes of reading disability.

### From the Schools

Reading clinics in various school systems: Philadelphia, Pennsylvania; St. Louis, Missouri; Duluth, Minnesota; New York, New York; and Detroit, Michigan.

## MEASURING PROGRESS

A schoolwide reading program is evaluated primarily by measuring students' achievement. This can be done by using standardized tests and informal teacher-made or textbook tests. In addition, we can evaluate a program by the student's grade on his report card—higher grades indicate greater achievement. This is the accepted method of evaluation. But these are external methods of measurement and convenient administrative yardsticks used to "place" students in a group or class.

## THE STUDENT MEASURES PROGRESS

Perhaps more attention should be given to self-appraisal, since much of the responsibility for improvement in reading rests with the student himself. In a paper presented at a conference on the role of tests in reading (at the University of Delaware, March 1960) Emmet Betts stated that a student should be able to evaluate his reading by asking himself if he can *think in a reading situation.* "Information on the pupil's thinking abilities includes an inventory of his concepts of time, space, quantity, etc.; of his abilities to state and hold clearly in mind the purpose of reading; to evaluate relevance of ideas in relation to purpose and to draw conclusions; to classify and index ideas in order to understand levels of abstraction and to apply these learnings to outlining and other means of organizing ideas effectively, as in the interpretation of definite and indefinite terms, identification of signals to ideas, and so on. All other facets of reading instruction are means to an end, and that end is comprehension, or understanding. A direct means to that end is a process called thinking."

The student who chooses books to read for the pleasure of reading is developing a "habit of reading" rather than reading to meet class assignments. Is this not a measure of reading achievement? One teacher has said that he measures reading improvement by the student's *library card* rather than his *report card* (and in most instances, this teacher observed, the number of books checked out on the library card was in direct ratio to school grades). Perhaps the student should use his library card as his personal report card.

Some schools have found that students like to use a self-appraisal check list to record their own progress. Table 1 is one example of such an informal device. The reading skills that will be covered during the school year are listed; the student checks his own progress in the appropriate column.

## THE TEACHER MEASURES PROGRESS

A schoolwide reading program is evaluated by measuring change in teachers as well as in students. It is expected that teachers who take courses, read the literature of the field, and who actively participate in in-service programs will experience changes in their teaching practices. "It is expected." But does it happen: to what extent, and for what period of time? Perhaps, as with students, the best "measurer" of this is the reading teacher himself.

Guides have been developed to help teachers evaluate their reading practices. The guide shown in Table 2 was developed by McInnes and Good for a study of the processes of effecting change in teachers' reading practices. This type of guide can serve as a check list as well as a self-evaluation instrument and might be used at the beginning of the term and then rechecked at the end of the term to see if, how often, and in what areas, change has occurred.

Measuring progress is a hazardous task. Just when we think we have succeeded in helping a youngster master a skill, we find that he becomes weak in another. Just as we feel that a youngster is galloping ahead, we suddenly find that lethargy sets in. Perhaps we tend to try to measure progress "too soon" with too discrete instruments. It was a wise youngster who, when asked what progress he thought he was making, replied, "I'm still sliding up the ladder."

## Table 1
### STANDARD READING REQUIREMENT FORM

| READING SKILL | SKILL NEEDED | SKILL ACHIEVED |
|---|---|---|
| *Word Recognition* | | |
| 1. Basic sight words.......................................... | | |
| 2. Phonic analysis | | |
| Single consonants........................................ | | |
| Consonant blends........................................ | | |
| Single vowels............................................ | | |
| Vowel combinations...................................... | | |
| 3. Structural analysis | | |
| Compound words........................................ | | |
| Root words.............................................. | | |
| Prefixes and suffixes..................................... | | |
| Contractions............................................. | | |
| Syllabication............................................ | | |
| Accent.................................................. | | |
| 4. Context clues............................................ | | |
| *Comprehension* | | |
| 1. Word and sentence meanings.............................. | | |
| 2. Main idea............................................... | | |
| 3. Details................................................. | | |
| 4. Classification........................................... | | |
| 5. Inferences.............................................. | | |
| 6. Follow directions........................................ | | |
| 7. Appreciation skills....................................... | | |
| *Work-Study* | | |
| 1. Parts of book........................................... | | |
| 2. Dictionary.............................................. | | |
| 3. Outlining; summarizing................................... | | |

## Table 2

### READING-PRACTICE GUIDE

A STUDY OF THE PROCESSES OF EFFECTING CHANGE IN
TEACHERS' READING PRACTICES

*Directions: Read each item and place a check mark in the column which applies
to what you have done.*

| Reading Practice | I have done this often | I have done this occa-sionally | I have not done this | I have not done this but think I should |
|---|---|---|---|---|
| 1. Near the beginning of the reading lesson, have had the pupils decide why they are reading the material, e.g., for information, for amusement. | | | | |
| 2. Have told the pupils the purpose of the reading lesson, e.g., "Our purpose is to find out how to get meanings of words we don't know." | | | | |
| 3. Have examined the material in the textbooks I intend to use in a lesson to see what reading skills were required. | | | | |
| 4. Have provided easier books for the poorest readers when reading assignments were given to the whole class. | | | | |
| 5. Have taken the good readers together as a group for more difficult reading while the rest of the class worked independently. | | | | |
| 6. Have given a very good reader an assignment to do independently on more difficult reading materials. | | | | |
| 7. Have asked a slow-learning child a question I felt sure he could answer successfully. | | | | |
| 8. Have asked a bright child challenging inferential questions calling for reading "between the lines." | | | | |

## Table 2 (continued)

| Reading Practice | I have done this often | I have done this occa-sionally | I have not done this | I have not done this but think I should |
|---|---|---|---|---|
| 9. Have worked with a small group of children to help them with a skill they especially needed, e.g., using a glossary; outlining. | | | | |
| 10. Have taken one child aside for a few minutes to help him with words he did not recognize. | | | | |
| 11. Have had an individual child read to me to see what kind of difficulties he was having. | | | | |
| 12. Have provided for the poorest reader in the class a book which he could understand. | | | | |
| 13. When a child could not understand a word, have had him re-read a whole sentence to find helpful context clues. | | | | |
| 14. Have asked a child to tell how he got the meaning of a particular word without using the dictionary. | | | | |
| 15. Have asked a child to explain what words or ideas from the material suggested the answer he gave. | | | | |
| 16. Have taught children to find a sentence in a paragraph that suggests the main idea. | | | | |
| 17. Have made up assignments which gave the children practice in using the index and the table of contents. | | | | |
| 18. Have had children pick out the main idea and most important details in a paragraph to help them learn to outline material. | | | | |
| 19. Have used pictures and blackboard drawings to clarify the meaning of a word or idea. | | | | |

## Table 2 (continued)

| Reading Practice | I have done this often | I have done this occa-sionally | I have not done this | I have not done this but think I should |
|---|---|---|---|---|
| 20. Have asked a few questions before a silent reading assignment to make sure the children knew what they were looking for when they read. | | | | |
| 21. Have selected four or five key words from material, listed them on the blackboard, and discussed their pronunciation. | | | | |
| 22. Have had the children read material to themselves before they were asked to read it orally. | | | | |
| 23. Have told children they could learn to read better by attacking hard words in a variety of ways, such as looking for prefixes, suffixes, and roots; checking for context clues. | | | | |
| 24. Upon hearing a child's answer to a question based on reading, have asked another pupil a question such as, "What do you think about that answer?" | | | | |
| 25. Have picked up from a child's answer clues that he had misread a word, e.g., "northeast" for "north-west." | | | | |
| 26. Have given the whole class a vocabulary test composed of words drawn from the section of the textbook or reader they were about to use. | | | | |
| 27. Have watched for lip movements while everyone in class read silently. | | | | |
| 28. Have presented children with written instructions to discover whether they could read and follow directions. | | | | |

## Table 2 (continued)

| Reading Practice | I have done this often | I have done this occa-sionally | I have not done this | I have not done this but think I should |
|---|---|---|---|---|
| 29. Have made some notes about children who showed severe reading difficulties early in the term. | | | | |
| 30. Have had children keep charts of their scores on teacher-made reading tests to help them see improvement. | | | | |
| 31. Have used class time to have children tell about pertinent things they have read outside of school. | | | | |
| 32. Have asked children to bring interesting items from the newspaper to be used on the bulletin board. | | | | |
| 33. Have read aloud to the class books or other materials to add interest to their classroom work. | | | | |
| 34. Have talked about interesting and difficult words which arose in reading. | | | | |
| 35. Have praised children for using particularly appropriate words in speaking. | | | | |

## Table 3
## READING INVENTORY

*Diagnosis*

Do I administer a standardized test?

How do I use the results of standardized tests:
   Do I note subscores?
   Do I analyze types of errors?
   Do I go over errors with individual students?

Do I administer the informal textbook test at the beginning of each school year before I decide whether or not to establish groups?

Is the student's basal reader at his instructional level?

Am I aware of the frustration, instructional, and independent reading levels of each student?

During a silent reading lesson am I alert to lip movements, pointing, span of interest, rates of reading, signs of distress?

*Grouping*

Are provisions made for the atypical child: the more advanced reader and the slower reader?

Have I planned for interesting "more-to-do": activities for those children who complete work ahead of the group?

Have I given my class sufficient training in independent activities to enable each group to function smoothly?

*Instructional Procedures*

Do I have a definite aim for each lesson?

Are my pupils aware of their purpose in reading?

Are my aims and the pupils' sometimes different?

When introducing a new story in the basal reader, do I vary my approach?

Do I utilize children's own experiences, audio-visual aids, or records as devices for arousing interest in the lesson to follow?

What means have I devised to sustain the child's interest until the selection is completed?

Do I make provision for clearing up vocabulary and concept difficulties before the reading of the selection?

Have I provided for the varied word-attack skills: context clues, configuration clues, structural analysis, phonetic analysis?

What devices do I use to fix vocabulary? Authorities agree that one exposure is not sufficient. Meeting the word in many different situations is more effective than drilling on the same word in the same context.

Is the reading lesson planned long enough in advance to arrange for the gradual development of skills?

## Table 3 (continued)

Do I look for more than "word pronunciation" as an indication of vocabulary comprehension?

Does oral reading have a proper place in the program?
> Does it follow silent reading?
> Is it used as a diagnostic test?
> Is it used to foster enjoyment in a listening situation?
> Is it used as a check on comprehension?

Do I provide for follow-up activities in other curriculum areas that grow out of the reading situation?

Do I vary my type of question? In addition to the factual question do I use the inferential type which requires reading "between the lines"?

Do I provide time for the children to summarize what they have learned?

Do I provide for an occasional "reading for fun" period?

Do I take time to lead the children to see that words have beauty; that words can be fun?

Do I read to my children—stories, poetry, riddles, humorous incidents, short excerpts from good literature? Does my manner show that *I* enjoy the reading?

Do I encourage home reading? Do I arrange to have my class share their outside reading with one another?

Do I help my pupils to catch the emotional tone of the story? Personalizing incidents in the story will help to vitalize the reading assignment.

*Materials of Instruction*

Am I accumulating interesting and colorful illustrative material to aid in the motivation and clarification of my reading lessons?

Do I make use of charts to record children's cooperative stories, class plans, shared experiences? Do I try to include vocabulary needed for a basal reading lesson when making those charts?

Is the workbook used as a means of reinforcing needed skills?

Do I make use of materials other than the basal reader and workbook for instructional purposes?

Do I make sufficient use of the blackboard to illustrate a point?

Do I dramatize my library corner so that my pupils will be anxious to visit it?

Do I provide books on various levels of difficulty and interest?

Table 4

## GUIDE FOR APPRAISING THE SPECIAL READING PROGRAM

|  | *Yes* | *No* |
|---|---|---|
| **A. *Physical Arrangement*** | | |
| 1. Does the seating arrangement lend itself to meeting the needs of individual and group teaching? | _____ | _____ |
| 2. Is the size of the room adequate? | _____ | _____ |
| 3. Are the storage facilities adequate? | _____ | _____ |
| 4. Is there evidence of physical provision for varied centers of interest? (E.g., bulletin boards; space for charts) | _____ | _____ |
| 5. Is there adequate chalkboard space? | _____ | _____ |
| 6. Are there open bookcases, magazine racks? | _____ | _____ |
| 7. Is the room attractive in appearance? (E.g., plants, pictures, charts) | _____ | _____ |
| **B. *Appraisal of Testing*** | | |
| 1. Does the teacher use standardized tests? | _____ | _____ |
| a. Diagnostic | _____ | _____ |
| b. Achievement | _____ | _____ |
| c. Intelligence | _____ | _____ |
| 2. Is there evidence of continued evaluation? | _____ | _____ |
| 3. Is there evidence of informal testing? | _____ | _____ |
| **C. *Materials*** | | |
| 1. Do the children have access to a typewriter? | _____ | _____ |
| 2. Are audio-visual materials used? | _____ | _____ |
| 3. Are supplementary reading materials used? (E.g., periodicals; extensive reading materials) | _____ | _____ |
| **D. *Skills and methods*** | | |
| 1. Is provision made for the sequential development of the various skills? | _____ | _____ |
| a. Word attack | _____ | _____ |
| b. Comprehension | _____ | _____ |
| c. Work-study | _____ | _____ |
| 2. Is reading integrated with the various curriculum areas? | _____ | _____ |
| 3. Are assignments provided on differential levels? | _____ | _____ |
| **E. *Planning*** | | |
| 1. Is there any evidence of planning for: | | |
| a. Individual needs | _____ | _____ |
| b. Small-group needs | _____ | _____ |
| c. Whole-class needs | _____ | _____ |

## Table 4 (continued)

|  | *Yes* | *No* |
|---|---|---|
| 2. Is there evidence of planning for varied activities within the period? | _____ | _____ |
| 3. Is there evidence of teacher-prepared materials to meet individual or group needs? | _____ | _____ |
| 4. Is there provision for periodic conferences between: | | |
|    a. Teacher and pupil | _____ | _____ |
|    b. Reading teacher and subject teacher | _____ | _____ |
|    c. Teacher and parent | _____ | _____ |
|    d. Reading teacher and guidance department | _____ | _____ |
| 5. Does the classroom management provide for the most efficient use of class time? | _____ | _____ |

F. *Community relations*

|  | | |
|---|---|---|
| 1. Is there provision for a working relationship with parents? | _____ | _____ |
| 2. Have provisions been made to promote the understanding and enlist the cooperation of community groups? | _____ | _____ |
| 3. Are community resources available and utilized? | _____ | _____ |
|    a. Library | _____ | _____ |
|    b. Community centers | _____ | _____ |
|    c. Field trips | _____ | _____ |
|    d. Others | _____ | _____ |

# GUIDES TO MEASURING PROGRESS

## In the Literature

Blusmer, Emery P. "Methods of Evaluating Progress of Retarded Readers in the Remedial Reading Program." In the 15th Yearbook of the National Council on Measurements Used in Education (New York: The Council, 1958), pp. 128–34.

A listing and short critique of various methods of evaluation.

"Evaluation of Three Methods of Teaching Reading—7th Grade," *Journal of Educational Research*, Vol. 54 (May 1961), pp. 356–58.

The three methods are: (1) individualized approach using a variety of materials; (2) individualized approach using SRA Reading Laboratories; and (3) conventional "one textbook" approach.

Thorndike, Robert L. *Concepts of Over- and Underachievement* (New York: Bureau of Publications, Teachers College, Columbia University, 1963).

Some precautions on setting up or evaluating achievement testing programs.

Turner, Richard L., and Father, Nicholas A. "Skill in Teaching, Assessed on the Criterion of Problem Solving," *Bulletin of the School of Education* (Bloomington, Ind.: Indiana University, 1961).

Suggests that teachers can assess their performance by viewing their reactions to specific problems. The instrument developed for this approach is worth studying.